ACADEMIC

OUTSIDER

Stories of Exclusion and Hope

VICTORIA REYES

stanford briefs
An Imprint of Stanford University Press
Stanford, California

Stanford University Press
Stanford, California

©2022 by Victoria Reyes. All rights reserved.

No part of this book may be reproduced or transmitted in any form
or by any means, electronic or mechanical, including photocopying
and recording, or in any information storage or retrieval system
without the prior written permission of Stanford University Press.

Printed in the United States of America on acid-free,
archival-quality paper

Library of Congress Cataloging-in-Publication Data available
on request.

Library of Congress Control Number: 2022013242

ISBN 9781503632998 (paper)
ISBN 9781503633681 (ebook)

Cover design: Rob Ehle
Cover image: Shutterstock

Typeset by Classic Typography in 11/15 Adobe Garamond

CONTENTS

Preface   *vii*

Academic Outsider   1

On Love and Worth   17

Conditional Citizenship   39

Living in Precarity   60

Overlapping Shifts and COVID-19   82

Academic Justice   104

Acknowledgments   *131*
Notes   *133*

PREFACE

Writing this book was cathartic. I would not have written it before the ongoing COVID-19 global pandemic started shutting down schools in March 2020. Nor would I have written it now that my kids have returned to in-person school. But for that year and a half, writing these essays was one of my only outlets. A place where I could pour out my thoughts, feelings, and frustrations as everything around me was crumbling.

Publishing it terrifies me.

It terrifies me precisely because, as an academic, our professional reputations precede us, shaping opportunities and access. In that sense, our professional reputations are all that we have. I fear that this book is a torpedo that I'm aiming toward my own future. And once I release it, my career will burst into flames, destroying any chance of achieving the kind of success that I've long desired. I've assumed that success means a professorship—maybe an endowed chair—at a top institution where I can pursue the kind of research I want with seemingly unlimited resources. But that is likely off the table now, especially within a sociology department—my disciplinary home. That's because, by publishing this book, I run the risk of being seen as someone who is "not serious." Instead, they'll put me in the box with other so-called angry or outspoken faculty of color. I'll be categorized as someone who doesn't conduct "rigorous" sociological research; who will only be a problem; a "troublemaker" who shares the academy's dirty secrets.

But maybe I was already there. At some point during the pandemic, it occurred to me that those scholars who will lose respect for me or judge me as "less than" after reading or even hearing about this book likely didn't respect me or my work to begin with and will only use this book as evidence as to why. And that is the problem.

So I'm letting this book out in the world. Because I should, but also because I have to. Once this book seeped out of me, there was no putting it back, even if that's what I wanted.

Higher education is a massive industry worldwide. One that the US has dominated for a long time. The US is a central destination for prospective students, faculty, and staff across the globe, with over a million international students enrolled each year in universities and colleges from 2015 to 2020.[1] In 2018 alone, these students contributed $44.7 billion to the US economy.[2] The US is also a dominating force of education through international branch campuses; 86 and counting US universities have satellites around the world, which constitutes approximately 28% of all international branch campuses globally, more than any other country.[3]

Higher education is also an industry that is deeply misunderstood by many people, especially laypeople and politicians on the right. Many of them see universities and colleges as hotbeds of "liberal" ideas about diversity, equity, and inclusion. Others assume that academia is a place where the main responsibility of faculty is to teach, with summers off and plenty of free time.

Neither characterization is accurate.

Academia is a workplace. Like many other workplaces, it's demanding and hierarchical, a place where people jockey over status, prestige, and resources. It's also steeped in racism, sexism, and other forms of hate and discrimination. Indeed, scholars have long documented the racism, sexism, and elitism that form the foundation of the academy. Which isn't to say that marginalized people haven't participated in the academy; it's just that disciplinary cultures based on hierarchy and prestige have long rendered their contributions invisible or as "less than." My own field of sociology, for example, tends to not teach or include the historic contributions of Anna Julia Cooper and Ida B. Wells-Barnett alongside those of Marx, Weber, or Durkheim. Nor teach or include the contemporary brilliance of Kimberlé Crenshaw and Gloria Anzaldúa, for example. After over a century since his first book, *The Philadelphia Negro*, was published, W.E.B. Du Bois is only now beginning to be recognized and incorporated into mainstream and elite sociology.[4]

Scholars of color such as Evelyn Nakano Glenn, Patricia Hill Collins, Eduardo Bonilla-Silva, Mary Romero, and Aldon Morris have all served as presidents of the American Sociological Association, and each of their contributions to sociology is similarly laudable. Some have pointed to their incredible achievements to demonstrate how inclusive the discipline is and how it is centered around a critical sociology on gender and racial inequality. Yet, these claims ignore that the types of scholars who are hired at top institutions and receive the most funding, and the types of scholarship that are published in the top journals in the field, still reflect a sociology that is exclusionary. Indeed, it was these exclusions that led to the necessary emergence of interdisciplinary fields and departments, such as Ethnic Studies, African American / Black Studies, Asian American Studies, Latinx Studies, Native American Indian / Indigenous Studies, and Women and Gender Studies.[5]

Even as the academy has pushed people out, academic outsiders—racialized people who are unwelcomed in the academy—have fought for, and demanded, a way in.

This book follows in the footsteps of these bold academic outsiders. It is a feminist creed that doesn't assume a linear pathway to success because life is not lived linearly.[6] People grow and move forward, but they also experience setbacks. Each of these essays operate similarly, moving back and forth in time and in thought. The essays blend the personal with the professional because they cannot be separated. As Kieu-Linh Caroline Valverde and

Wei Ming Dariotis note in their edited volume on Asian American women faculty, "the oppression we study in society is the oppression we experience in academia; it is the same oppression."[7]

This book also takes seriously the multifaceted experience of being an outsider. Being an academic outsider is about the lived experience of being included or excluded from everyday hallway conversations, mentor and peer interactions, publications, and awards. It's when you don't see yourself reflected in the other people around you or in the scholarship you read. It's when your experiences and thoughts are discounted and dismissed, especially— or particularly—when they run afoul of the dominant position.

This book recognizes the multiple paths that result in being seen or treated as an outsider. In academia, when we talk about positionality—or how our social positions shape our experience in the world—we mostly discuss how our visible characteristics, like our race/ethnicity, relate to our research.[8] This is important. However, our lives contain multiple strands. We often experience being an outsider in ways that may have little to nothing to do with our research. Yet the structure of academia and our daily interactions with colleagues are steeped in processes and a culture that are, at least initially, inaccessible to those of us from outsider backgrounds.

In the pages that follow, I share some—but not all— aspects of my life. Yet this book is not meant to be a guide to self-actualization. Nor is it a plea for pity or to be exalted. I do not want to be someone that people can point to and say, "If she can do it, you can too." Nor is my aim to romanticize or valorize my and my family's pain, or to hold our story up as the Filipino American family, a tokenized story, something that Cathy Park Hong writes about in her book *Minor Feelings*.[9]

Instead, I use parts of my story as a jumping off point to talk about exclusion and participation in the academy. I write it to honor Audre Lorde's recognition that vulnerability and feelings are strengths.[10] My vulnerability throughout these pages is a strength, not a weakness—though it often doesn't feel that way—because my story contradicts myths that elevate professors as nonhumans who don't experience any hardship. Even if individual readers may not be able to relate to my personal experiences, they help remind those in power that the modern academy continues to be centered around white married men.

I want other academic outsiders to know that there are those of us within the academy who see them for who they are, not just as grad students (for example) who need to prove their worth. We academic outsiders know, and want others to know, that people with marginalized backgrounds are people worthy of respect who can contribute to our chosen disciplines in multiple ways. They are wanted and belong in the academy, despite daily messages to the contrary. I am but one of many scholars of color lifting one another up through their scholarship. My hope is that this book can serve, for those who may not know where to start, as a beginning archive of who these scholars are and what they've written, a starting point from which readers can delve into this vast literature.

It is also my hope that this book becomes obsolete, but I'm highly skeptical.

Contrary to popular belief, the academy is conservative and resistant to change. The faculty who are marginalized for their race, gender, sex, sexuality, and migration status have been fighting these battles for a long time. That means we're not alone, we have a foundation from which to build and people who have trailblazed—and continue to do so—the paths before us. We also have a long way to go.

What, then, to do? While there are books that can help us navigate grad school or the beginnings of the tenure track,[11] the rules of the game are ever evolving because our rank changes (from grad student to assistant professor, for example), as does the circle of who we interact with (such as the new people we meet at each conference we attend). Often, I am reminded that no matter how comfortable I start to feel, I'm an outsider.

So, here I am, writing this book, sharing my story. Why? And why now?

Advice rooted outside one's own lived experience can be exhausting to receive because it individualizes "other" people's situations. This book attempts to be different. It draws on feminist attempts to use the personal—my personal—to critique structures of power, in the lineage of essays and poems of writers like Maya Angelou, while simultaneously providing a mirror for others struggling down similar paths. The academy won't change overnight. Nor does change occur through purely demographic shifts, as Christine Williams notes.[12] It will only change when standard structures of knowledge and power are confronted. But in the academy, having access to the levers of change means getting through graduate school, the job market, and tenure. I'm hoping this book helps someone with that.

I have to admit that I've always struggled with writing personal statements precisely because it felt like I had to sell, or package, my life in a way I found deeply problematic. So, how did I get comfortable enough to publish some parts of my life I've only shared with my therapist? To be honest, I'm not sure. Books like *Thick and Other Essays* by Tressie McMillan Cottom,[13] *How To Be Less Stupid about Race* by Crystal M. Fleming,[14] *Eloquent Rage* by Brittney Cooper,[15] and *How to Be an Antiracist* by Ibram X. Kendi[16] are among the recent writings that blend the deeply personal with critique. They helped solidify my desire to write this book.

In the following personal essays, then, I'll illustrate the different facets of being an academic outsider, both as an act of recognition and as a call for change. In that respect, this book is not only for sociologists, social scientists, or anyone with a specific disciplinary affiliation. It's for anyone entering the academy, to show the challenges that may lie ahead, as well as for those who were pushed out of the academy or their own discipline, who may recognize their own experiences in mine. It's also for those graduate students, lecturers, and adjuncts struggling with the academic job market. When I was a grad student searching for a job, I oozed desperation. I want those readers to understand that our choices should not be, and should not have to be, made in desperation. Such a choice is not really a choice at all.

This book is also a plea for those of us on the tenure track to enact change where we can, to not repeat or enable what's harmful about our profession. It is also to remind those readers who already have tenure that graduate students, precarious faculty, and untenured faculty have varied life experiences that they may not understand. To show them how seemingly off-the-cuff or even well-intentioned remarks can signal to students, and even their colleagues, that they don't belong in the academy and never will, no matter what they do.

I hope my writings will be taken seriously, that those in power heed my call for change. But these writings also stem from a place that I can no longer contain. I finally have found a comfort and confidence in myself and who I am that I want to share with the world. As Sara Ahmed writes, "To get ready often means being prepared to be undone."[17] This is me, taking in a deep breath, plunging headfirst into sharing this manuscript with the world. Once it is published, it cannot be taken back. Here I go.

ACADEMIC OUTSIDER

ACADEMIC OUTSIDER

On the day of my wedding, my mother told me that she would go through everything again just to have me. I didn't believe her. It's only been in the years after her death that I can see how she loved me the best she could. She was, herself, broken. Filled with anger and mental anguish. Unable to stop herself from passing along the trauma etched into her stretchmarks. Her trauma was molded onto my features, reflected back on her every time she looked at me.

For as long as I can remember, I've always been an outsider. I didn't belong. Didn't fit neatly into any category. That was the message I got from classmates, strangers, and even my own family. Who I am, and my real relationship to everyone else, is a dirty family secret. I've spent my life on the periphery, always looking in but never wholly welcomed. Seeing life as a game, one I could never win.[1] Yet always trying to figure out how to play, in the hopes that one day, I could prove my worth.

That I could be accepted. But even to this day, I'm still being told in ways subtle and overt that I'm not quite enough.

When I was younger, this message took many forms. I was told by my grandmother's boyfriend that, while I might look Brown on the outside, on the phone I sounded like every other white girl. In family pictures, I'm out of place. My face is like one of those children's puzzles where you choose which one doesn't belong. With my mom and either of my stepfathers and their child(ren) when we were younger, I'm always the odd one out. The darker one. The same for photographs of me with my grandma and the relatives I was raised alongside—never looking like anyone. Always having to qualify my relationships with people. The picture of my grandma when she was younger, my mom when she was a toddler, and him. The person I get my nose from and my height. My oval face. For a long time, I had that picture framed. I'd stare at it, unable to help myself, searching for the similarities in our faces and wishing the obvious similarities weren't there.

Kids aren't subtle about drawing boundaries around social groups. During middle school, we went to Camp Kern for a team-building exercise. That day, I was the last one on my team to make it over an obstacle course wall. Each team was responsible for figuring out how everyone could get to the top without a rope. The camp counselor made a comment about how the group saved the heaviest for last. I was embarrassed. My body differed too much from those of the white girls in my class. In these instances, and others, I didn't belong; was never and *could never* be enough.

When I was recruited to the International Churches of Christ (ICOC), I thought I had found a place I belonged. There was even a set of Filipino American siblings, with a Filipina mother and white father, in the teen ministry. The church's set list of rigid rules appealed to me, gave me something to hold onto in the chaos that was my life. I was recruited the summer I was homeless, staying with my grandma's boyfriend's ex-wife. I tried my best to follow all the rules. I rose through the ranks of the teens and was "discipled" by the women's teen ministry evangelist. You confessed all your sins and thoughts to your discipler, who was supposed to hold you accountable and help you grow closer to God. The status of your discipler was also an indicator of your own status in the group. That the women's teen ministry leader was my discipler meant I had a relatively high status and more spiritual potential than my peers.

My attitude about the ICOC changed when I went to The Ohio State University for college. I attended Ohio State as an undergrad in part because of the strength of its campus ministry. Soon, though, I started asking questions that ultimately led me to one of the most difficult decisions I ever had to make: to leave an organization that many people (including myself) consider a fundamentalist evangelical cult. For months, even years, afterward, I would start having a panic attack whenever I saw someone from the church. Once I left, I no longer had anyone. No friends. No support system.

It was in the classroom—specifically Asian American Studies—that I finally found a place where I belonged. Felt secure. On more stable ground. I made the field a minor, which meant taking a set number of courses, including an independent reading course on Filipino America and a graduate seminar on Psychology of Filipino Americans. I joined the Pilipino Student Association (PSA) and acted as the liaison to the joint faculty and student Asian American Studies Committee. On this committee, I interacted with faculty and advocated with them for ethnic studies classes. I finally felt as though I had valuable contributions to share and what I had to say was important. I belonged.

At times, however, I still didn't quite feel like I fit in. I was taller than the other Filipino students. Had too "white" a nose. I didn't speak Tagalog (yet). I hadn't eaten and didn't crave Filipino food. Instead of Filipino food, growing up we would eat leftovers from Manchu Wok, a Chinese fast-food restaurant, that my grandma would bring home after she got off work there, one of her many jobs.

But in classes and in writing a thesis? That's where I thrived. Even when I found myself surprised that readings from the Philippines didn't appear on the syllabus of a Pacific Islander literature course, I was in an environment where faculty encouraged students to ask hard questions. My readings and writing centered on issues of power and critique. On puzzles. On searching for more information. Here, in these spaces, scholars of color questioned the norm and pushed back. Even if my own background wasn't represented, I felt like there was space for me to make it my own.

The "Asian American" or "Asian American Pacific Islander" (AAPI) label can be a hard fit for Filipinos. In the United States, this label is commonly used to refer to people from, or who have familial connections to, countries in East Asia. The term can be charged, sometimes used as a shorthand for the myth of the model minority, or the view that Asian Americans are "successful" minorities who have achieved high earnings and education, assimilated into the white US mainstream, and no longer face discrimination and racism due to their "culture."[2] But this association renders invisible the histories of empire, violence, and racial, gendered, and sexual subjugation and exploitation that Asian American people have experienced, as well as their varied histories, trajectories, migration pathways, and lived experiences.[3]

My own ambivalence about using the AAPI label to describe myself probably also stems from the fact that, outside of Filipino circles and the people that I know personally, I am not usually seen as fitting under that umbrella. Instead, I'm seen and coded as Latina. Sociologist Nancy López and colleagues use the term *street race* to refer to the race that people who don't know you would assume you are, based on what you look like.[4] I'm often greeted in Spanish, not only because of how I look but also because of my last name. Filipino American sociologist Anthony Ocampo writes about this in his book

Latinos of Asia, how many Filipino Americans often feel uneasy with the AAPI label, connecting instead with members of Latinx communities who share their history of Spanish colonialism.[5]

As an undergraduate, I remember being inspired by what I was reading: essays from *This Bridge Called My Back*, an anthology of writings by radical women of color edited by Cherríe Moraga and Gloria Anzaldúa; Gloria Anzaldúa's *Borderlands/La Frontera*; Yuri Kochiyama's memoir *Passing It On*; the critical essays in the anthology *Pinay Power*, edited by Melinda L. de Jesús; Haunani-Kay Trask's *From a Native Daughter*; the essays in the anthology *Asian/Pacific Islander American Women*, edited by Shirley Hune and Gail Nomura, and so many others. When I arrived in grad school, I was surprised to learn that these types of writings were not taught in classes. They didn't appear on the reading lists, and none of the faculty incorporated their insights into their research.

It was only after I received my PhD that I ventured back into Asian American Studies, Ethnic Studies, women of color feminisms, and much of the scholarship that initially drew me into academia. In particular, I've been drawn to Black Feminist Thought: the dilemmas Anna Julia Cooper faced in being confronted by segregated bathrooms and not knowing which to choose; learning to embrace differences among women of color and use my anger to better society, as Audre Lorde teaches; bell hooks's insights into teaching critical thinking and how love cannot coexist with desires for power and domination. Inspired by Patricia Hill Collins's observations that being an outsider within the academy can allow our creativity to flourish and provides critical insight into various forms and experiences of systems of oppression. Drawing on Kimberlé Crenshaw's understanding of intersectionality, how systems of oppression based on race, class, and gender intersect to shape different experiences for women of color (particularly Black women).

Although I am not a Black feminist, cannot produce Black Feminist Thought, and do not experience the world and systems of oppression in the same way as Black women, acceptance of the messiness of life, structural positions as outsiders, deep concern with how these positions and accompanying lived experiences are shaped by broader structures, and calls for solidarity and to act with integrity all speak to me. I find parallels between my life and those writings, conversations, and friendships with Black feminist scholars. In their spaces, I am honored to be a guest. I feel welcomed despite, or maybe because of, my differences.

Most of us are outsiders in one way or another. We are seen and felt as different than those around us. As not belonging. This book is for other outsiders, those who do not conform. Those who, as Audre Lorde writes in her book whose title I honor with this essay and manuscript, are outside the "mythical norm [where] the trappings of power reside."[6]

In the United States, Lorde writes, "this norm is usually defined as white, thin, male . . . heterosexual, Christian and financially secure."[7] If you are not all of these, you are an outsider in some way. Yet, it's also important to recognize that not all outsiders experience being an outsider the same way, whether because of racism, sexism, misogynoir,[8] xenophobia, or other systems of exclusion. Being excluded is not a dichotomous label: it is not the case that you are either an outsider (in whatever avenue) or not. Seeing exclusion as dichotomous would diminish the experience of what Patricia Hill Collins describes as "outsider[s]-within"— people within a social space but in the margins.[9] Always on the periphery. Never accepted due to gendered racism. Just like identities,[10] being an outsider is experienced along a continuum that is racialized, gendered, classed, and embodied. It's fluid, situational and context dependent.

The importance of lived experiences is one of the main insights of Black Feminist Thought and women of color feminisms, from Anna Julia Cooper's *A Voice from the South* (1892) to Zakiya Luna and Whitney N. Laster Pirtle's *Black Feminist Sociology* (2021), and so many other writings, from academic books and journals to poetry to music to fiction and nonfiction books. This emphasis is also one that José Itzigsohn and Karida Brown identify as one of the key tenets of Du Boisian sociology, which is "a sociological approach that draws from the theoretical and methodological tradition of W.E.B. Du Bois and puts racism and colonialism at the center of the understanding of modernity."[11] In *Souls of Black Folk,* Du Bois writes, "between me and the other world there is ever an unasked question . . . How does it feel to be a problem? I answer seldom a word. And yet, being a problem is a strange experience, —peculiar even for one who has never been anything else."[12] He describes how, as a Black boy, he came to understand his Blackness after a particular encounter with a white girl: "It dawned upon me with a certain suddenness that I was different from others; or like, mayhap, in heart and life and longing but shut out from their world by a vast veil."[13] No matter what he did, he was marked as other, while the white people he encountered remained unmarked.[14] Experiencing life by juxtaposing the knowledge of white society with the invisibility of, and the systems of oppressions that shaped, himself and Black society. These concepts are rooted in Blackness, Black experiences, enslavement, and anti-Black racism. For Black people in the US, double consciousness and the veil are cultural touchstones.

The idea of an invisible barrier separating "us" from "them," being always on the outside, forever seeing but not fully being a part of that other side: this resonates with those of us who are Brown racialized outsiders.[15] A veil also shrouds our vision, though the veil may not be as thick and may be more porous than it is for Black peoples. We can see through to the other side, but the veil masks us and marks us, our knowledge, and our experiences as fundamentally different. Our own double consciousness is always aware that we're marked, that we live through the eyes of those who are not. Sociologist Neda Maghbouleh, herself Iranian American, writes that "whiteness is fickle and volatile—and, more often than not, revoked in the mundane and ordinary interactions that make up the everyday politics of race."[16]

To be an *academic outsider* is to be separated from other academics, and from university life more generally, by our lived experiences. Our lives do not mirror those for whom the walls of the academy were built. Elijah Anderson uses the term *white spaces* to refer to the perceptual categorization of spaces based on the overwhelming proportion of white people there.[17] He compares the overwhelming number of white people in these spaces to the relative absence of Black people, who, when present, "reflexively note the proportion of whites to blacks, or may look around for other blacks with whom to commune if not bond . . . when judging a setting as too white, they can feel uneasy and consider it to be informally 'off limits.'" White people, meanwhile, typically see these same spaces as "unremarkable, or as normal, taken-for-granted reflections of civil society."[18] In my experience, Brown people often reflexively think and experience white spaces in similar ways to Black people.

Today, as a Brown woman in the academy, I continue to experience moments that mark me as an outsider. Academia, the world of intellectual exchange, should be a safe space, but make no mistake: the academy is a white space. A white workplace, where racialized, gendered, and sexual outsiders are constantly reminded that our presence in the academy is contingent and in constant flux. For me, these reminders often take the form of being coded as Brown and immigrant-adjacent. When I occasionally forget how I am marked, I am often soon reminded, jarred back to the reality of my outside status.

The structures of the social world in which we live weren't built for us outsiders. They do not resemble our lives. Take for example, the time I was chatting with two other Filipinx scholars at a Sociologists for Women in Society conference hotel. On one side of us were the elevators; on the other, seats where you could order food and drinks. We were discussing whether my children call my grandma "Gaga" because of its Filipino meaning of "mischievous" (I had no idea and when I asked my grandma, she said "I don't know"). A blond waitress walking by overheard us and commenting, "FYI, it's pronounced 'mis-che-vous.'" Intruding into our private conversation to "correct" our pronunciation of the word as she moved past.

In the academy, being coded as a mother of color means being dismissed. I remember the time I was pregnant and attending a talk in our department's colloquium series. During the Q&A, a male graduate student asked a question that wasn't quite fully developed, but the speaker, a white man, gave his full attention to it, elaborating on both the question and how his work answers it. When I stood up next, my third-trimester belly was obvious to everyone. My question received a one-sentence, dismissive reply before the speaker turned and called on the next person (another white man).

"Hepeating," "mansplaining," and "whitesplaining"[19] are all familiar experiences to me and other racialized outsiders: we say something that is ignored until the idea is praised when it is repeated by someone else—a man, often a white man. The examples could go on.

I fully recognize I may not, at first glance, appear to be an outsider or outsider-within. I hold a PhD from a top graduate program, a tenure-track job at a research university, have published solo-authored publications, and my work has been recognized with grants, fellowships, and awards. I see and acknowledge those forms of privileges. Despite this, I do not experience the academy as an insider.

Even as I came to the academy via a literature that centered the life experiences of people who looked like me, my graduate training taught me, in both formal and informal lessons, that elite scholars look and act certain ways. Drenched in an awareness of how people evaluate scholars, there's a drive in me that hungers to publish in top disciplinary journals, get a job at a top-ranked department, and get more awards. I somehow still believe that all of those things will satiate my deep-rooted need and longing. I don't want to be considered just "good enough," because of, or considering, my background. I want to be "good enough" compared to anyone. Yet, that part of me wars with another part, one that recognizes where I've come from and how far I've come. One that recognizes the inequity of academia and takes seriously the need to dismantle it in whatever ways I'm able. To continue paving the way ahead of me, as so many have done before. This book is a step on that path.

Although it comes at great cost, growing up as an outsider turns out to be good training to become an ethnographer.[20] I was constantly watching life from the outside, trying to understand the rules of the game and move my way through. Hoping that, if I only learned the rules of the game and did everything right, then I would be more accepted. I applied the same strategy to navigating the academy, entering graduate school, applying for postdoctoral fellowships, and settling into a tenure-track job. I've learned (and continue to learn as each stage in the career of an academic involves a learning curve because of new responsibilities) the rules: which journals to publish in to "matter," the hierarchies of the field, what constituted a "good" job. I primarily learned these lessons among graduate students and between faculty and graduate students in informal conversations in hallways and at conferences. And from keen observation.

It takes a lot of work, observation, and thought to figure things out. Combining critical race theory with Bourdieu, Tara Yosso calls these "skills of maneuvering through social institutions" *navigational capital*.[21] In some ways, the academy rewards outsiders with navigational capital. Those with skills of observation, who notice the world around them. Those who are drawn to reading. To writing. Ideas. Those who have a dedication to the discovery of the world, often at the expense of other pursuits.

Yet the academy is only made for certain types of outsiders. We know that many academics are from families with relatively more wealth and more education than others. For example, in a study of over 7,218 tenure-stream faculty members in PhD-granting universities across eight disciplines, Allison C. Morgan and colleagues found that over half of them had parents with a master's degree or higher and nearly a quarter have at least one parent who holds a PhD.[22] This was even more pronounced when they examined the family backgrounds of faculty working at more prestigious departments, where "faculty at these elite departments are 53.6% more likely to have a parent who holds a PhD than are faculty at the least prestigious departments."[23] We also know that modern academic work was created and formed around white men. And that faculty and universities are both forces of empire. And that peer review—how others assess the worth and value of your scholarship—replicates the same hierarchical biases that pervade the rest of our society. In that respect, the academic workplace is a world unto itself, with its own insiders and outsiders. Its own rules. Where people fight for resources and status for themselves and those like them, leaving others on the margins.

One outcome of all my work in learning the academy's formal and informal rules is that I've become the consummate academic. I've tried to do everything "right." But knowing and following the rules isn't enough. I am continually confronted with my status as a racialized and gendered academic, with the knowledge that neither my work nor my being will ever be enough.

Bedelia Nicola Richards argues that research that explores how people use educational knowledge to succeed (cultural capital) is rooted in a class-based master narrative that centers whiteness and white people's experiences and knowledge.[24] This literature, she argues, posits a "deficit perspective" in which Black and Brown people don't have enough _____ of something or were not taught _____, and that is the reason they are unsuccessful. From this perspective, educational inequality will be eliminated, and equity achieved, if only Black, Brown, and Indigenous peoples knew the correct information and how to appropriately navigate institutes of higher learning. This is where the advice books come in to help level the playing field regarding knowledge (or cultural capital) behind the "hidden curriculum"—the unwritten rules of the academy.[25] But this knowledge is precisely *partial* because life is not just about learning the rules of the game (cultural capital). It's about lived experience and what we embody—the "feel" of the game, what social theorist Pierre Bourdieu calls *habitus*.[26] It's also about the generational traumas (and joys) that are passed onto us and etched into our skins.

The rules are not the same for everyone. During my period of advice-giving, I thought that they may have been. Or at least, I thought that people like me could succeed by following them. In contrast, Richards calls for a race-conscious framework that centers those who are marginalized. She urges researchers to think through and theorize the uses and forms of cultural capital. She is right. The focus on navigating the game,[27] for better or for worse, can distract us from the fact that the game itself is rigged—already set up to fail most of us no matter what we do. What needs to change are not the behaviors of those most vulnerable, but rather the broader structures and foundations of the academy. The academy's most basic assumptions about value and worth need to be radically transformed if Black and Brown scholars are to truly feel a part of it—not as tokens, but as valued and respected members.

"I wish you had never been born. I should have had an abortion."

I can't remember the first time my mother told me that. But I do remember the first time I responded differently than either freezing in place or bursting into tears.

We were living in the Mason-Montgomery house. We moved constantly and were never in the same place for too long, so I called our house by the name of the street where it was located, to give myself roots. Sometimes we were evicted; other times, I'm not quite sure why we moved. There's the Jefferson Avenue house, the Mason-Montgomery house. The Cowan Drive apartment. The Kings Mills apartment. Mason Road. Most of these places fell in the same school district, so only once did I change schools. There was also the one summer we were briefly homeless, and I stayed with my grandma's boyfriend's ex-wife.

I remember the white door of the Mason-Montgomery house. Just a few doors down from the local cemetery, and across the street from a corn field. It sat on a slight hill. My uncle's car slid down that hill when it snowed one winter. In response, my grandma's boyfriend threw a chair. The house's white door sticks in my mind because my uncle's daughter drew on it with crayon, right before a visit from our landlord, upsetting my grandma's boyfriend again. We were eventually evicted.

On the day I spoke back to my mother, we had gotten into a fight. Since we lived on Mason-Montgomery, I must have been in junior high. My mother stormed past me as she yelled those words.

I had an inkling of what must have happened. Not having a father. Raised by my grandmother, alongside her other children. Everything about me and my identity shrouded in secrecy. My tumultuous relationship with my mother . . .

I yelled back, "What were you, raped?"

My mother froze and then stormed out that white door, into the sunlight. I collapsed in tears, like I always did whenever we fought, which was most of the time. Most of the time, that is, when we saw each other. I've lived with my grandma since I was born. My mother was only fifteen years old when she had me. When I was about seven, I tried to live with her for a year or so. The experiment failed.

There were a lot of us there at the three-and-a-half bedroom Mason-Montgomery house: my grandma, my grandma's boyfriend, my aunt Lisa (who was four years older than me), one of my uncles (who was five years older than

me), his girlfriend, their daughter, and a Chinese immigrant man who was my grandma's and my boss at a Chinese fast-food place where I worked under the table. He
lived in the basement. During the weekends, my grandma's boyfriend's two daughters came over. One was a year
younger than my aunt, and she had her own bed in the
room that she shared with Lisa. The other was my age,
and she had a bed in my room, which rolled under my
bed when she wasn't there. I had no privacy. To get upstairs,
you had to walk through my room. There was not even a
door that separated the upstairs hallway from my room,
though there was one between my room and the rest of
the main floor. But it didn't lock. I remember the large
wardrobe that was the only other piece of furniture in my
bedroom because when the second bed was popped out,
there wasn't any more space. I hid inside the wardrobe
one April Fool's Day, hoping to scare my grandma into
thinking I ran away. Pranking, or scaring, one another on
April Fool's Day was a way we showed our love. But after
a while, when no one called my name or seemed to realize I wasn't around, I left my wardrobe to see what was
going on. My grandma and Lisa were on the phone trying to prank others. I was forgotten.

In that moment, after my mother stormed out the
front door, I felt unloved. Unlovable. The first time I can
remember feeling that way came at age seven. It's a time
that anchors me in place: the Jefferson Avenue house.
Here, one uncle had the primary room. I remember his
waterbed and always feeling like his room was off-limits,

I couldn't enter. My other uncle had his own room with bunk beds. When she wasn't at one of her three jobs, Grandma slept on the couch in the living room, something I didn't realize until I was much older. Lisa, another aunt, and I all shared the third bedroom. Lisa had a daybed that was placed against the wall. She had a porcelain baby doll that you could pull the string and music would play. I remembered I loved to hold on to it. I would hear the music and twirl around, making myself dizzy. I slept on a mattress against another wall with my other aunt. One uncle had boxing gloves, and sometimes we'd use the mattress as a boxing ring. I could never win. But the day that anchors me to the Jefferson Avenue house, I woke up in the middle of the night, being touched. Years later, when I told my grandmother what happened, she replied that the person was probably dreaming. It was an accident. I shouldn't think about it.

But I did. Her seemingly offhanded remark planted in me seeds of fear that I would do the same. One more reason to not want kids: to not pass on my genes and to avoid doing things in my sleep, without even knowing. Even today, when I co-sleep with one or both of my kids, I make sure we have separate blankets or sheets, and I try to have a pillow in between us.

I remember another time, when that aunt asked to borrow the money that I kept in my neon pink purse. I saved up all the coins I could find in that purse. They were mostly pennies. She asked to borrow the money that was in it and to not tell anyone. She promised to pay it back. I can't remember how long it was before I told my grandma—it could have been a day, a week or a month—and I can't remember why I told her. But I do remember, shortly after telling her, that aunt was arrested. Went to jail. I thought it was my fault. I made a mistake. Telling on her wasn't worth her getting arrested and leaving. I would later find out she had stolen money from her job.

I was fourteen when I committed my first "suicidal gesture." That's the step between suicidal thoughts and a suicide attempt. It wouldn't be my last. And I don't quite know what kept pulling me back. Probably my grandma. Eventually, my significant other, my kids. But really, what's made all the difference is the years, decades, of talk therapy and medication. Actively working with professionals to not have this struggle at the forefront of my mind and to not have suicide be a viable option. Working toward self-acceptance. Realizing my worth. Brainstorming strategies on how to handle life.

But realizing my worth is a struggle in and of itself. A mixture of self-hatred, anger, and worthlessness is etched on my bones from my childhood. If my own mother couldn't love me, who could? What more could I do? My nose. My height. My wide shoulders someone in middle school once commented on, telling me they were so wide I could play football. Who knows what else? All carrying the telltale signs of my father. A rapist. And worse: while unrelated to her, my mother's rapist was the father of her siblings. In public, I refer to the kids I grew up with as my uncles and aunts. And they are that, though when talking with family, I just use their first name. That's because we grew up together and we're close in age. They are also my half-siblings. But we never talk about that.

Many—too many—women of color, Indigenous women, immigrant women, poor women, white women, trans women, women whose identities intersect these categories, and others, share histories, especially family histories, of sexual violence. This is not a new story. It's been going on for centuries and continues today.[1] And this sexual violence tells women, implicitly, that we are unworthy of being safe.

For me, the message that I was unloved and unlovable came first, and loudest, from my mother. But every time we're rejected, treated differently, or dismissed, whether by our families, our communities, or our social institutions, we're being told that we're unloved and unworthy. When states and cities don't invest in public schools, when managers treat their workers with suspicion, when authority figures discount our experiences because of our race, gender, or sexuality,[2] we're being told that we do not deserve their investments of time, money, and attention. Whether we're talking about relationships, family, or society writ large, the experience of being loved is rooted in recognition and resources. Being denied those resources and recognition marks us as unloved, the essence of what it means to be an outsider.

How we understand and assess ourselves is filtered through the eyes of others.[3] In her essay collection *Thick*, Tressie

McMillan Cottom declares that she is unattractive or ugly. She tells readers that she's not internalizing the dominant culture's assessment of her. Instead, she's thinking through beauty as capital, "naming what has been done to" her and "signaling who did it."[4]

Love, too, is a form of capital.

Love is an emotion—a feeling of care, whether it be romantic, sexual, friendly, or familial.[5] And these feelings of love spur action, organize our thinking,[6] and permeate popular culture, from songs and movies to television shows and toys. Love is so powerful that states intensely regulate love and its corollary, lust. In the United States, interracial marriages have only been legal since 1967, when the US Supreme Court struck down a Virginia law prohibiting the interracial marriage of Mildred Loving and Richard Loving. Love also has been central to organizing international political economies. Bars and clubs frame which kinds of sexual activity are desirable and obtainable, the communities we live and work in frame which types of relationships are appropriate, and which are not, and governments and militaries regulate, organize, and criminalize particular kinds of intimacies, such as sex work and marriages.

But what would it mean to see love as a form of capital? When sociologists refer to capital, they're often drawing on the social theory of Pierre Bourdieu,[7] who discusses different forms of capital. Scholars have also used the term *capital* to study our feelings. Emotional capital refers to the emotional resources, skills, and energies that people acquire and use, strategically and actively, in their lives.[8]

So, emotions are not just feelings or only the "stuff" of culture. As a form of capital, emotions shape relationships and individuals' access to a whole set of resources (or their absence). But let's zoom out. What if instead of looking at the ways that individuals draw on, or teach others, emotional resources and skills—that is, instead of seeing emotions solely as a form of capital that people do or do not have—we emphasize how emotions *shape* and are *constitutive* of capital and our decisions regarding how resources are used and distributed and where we put our labor and energy? What if we also see love as a bundle of practices associated with our labor?

Let's break the concept down. To love or to care also means to invest, whether the thing being invested is time, money, or something else. Here's an example. It's often taken for granted that people love their families. What does that mean? Traditionally it means that, to the extent that you are able, you provide shelter and food for your closest relations, send children to school, and treat them nicely—whether that's kissing a "boo-boo," rocking them to sleep, reading to them, celebrating their accomplishments, or encouraging them in their passions.

For many caregivers, parents or otherwise, "loving your family" also means personal sacrifice, which usually means working long hours and putting the needs of others first. In the case of many—particularly Filipina women—it also means leaving children behind, migrating to another country to work (often as domestic workers).[9] Spending money to buy, or sending money for others to buy, things like food, clothes, electronics, necessities is another way that caregivers demonstrate love.

Sociologist Viviana Zelizer[10] talks about how people match *what* we give to *whom* based on our relationships, which are shaped by feelings.[11] That is, a favored child may receive more attention or toys than a less-favored child. When we're angry with, dislike, or hate someone, we may withhold resources from them and limit our loved ones' interactions and access to them. The emotions available to us, and our ability to use them, are also shaped by historical processes and structural conditions.[12]

In this respect, love—like all forms of capital—is also unequal. Our default focus on individual or family sacrifices as signs of a parent's love masks structural inequalities. Not everyone can provide for their child(ren). Some people must leave their children behind and move to another country to better their children's lives. But that's not necessarily because of a lack of love. It's because of power and inequality. It's about how structural racism, sexism, classism, and legacies of colonialism shape who is deemed worthy or unworthy of resources. For some parents, leaving their children is the only way to provide for them.

The question of who is loved, worthy, and thus, deserving—and who is deemed unlovable, unworthy, and undeserving—is political and has long gripped social scientists because the answer has very real socioeconomic and political consequences.[13] The intense debates in the US about reproductive rights, including both abortion and forced sterilization, for example, gestures to the link between worthiness and resources. Beginning in the early twentieth century, for example, many US states operated eugenics programs that ultimately sterilized tens of thousands of people without their consent, mostly women of color and people with disabilities.[14] The practice of forced sterilization inspired the Nazis and continues today: a September 2020 whistleblower complaint by Dawn Wooten, a nurse, alleged "seemingly high numbers of hysterectomies performed on immigrants detained at [the US Immigration and Customs Enforcement facility in Ocilla, Georgia], which was followed by stories of multiple women being sterilized without their consent."[15] Both now and in 1920, the practice of forced sterilization is rooted in eugenics—that is, in racist policies that turn social and biological ideas about whose life is worth living into a form of population control.

We typically think of eugenics, with its emphasis on forced sterilization, as having a different politics than abortion restrictions. And yet, both eugenics and abortion are about racialized, gendered, and sexed notions of worth. Beginning in 1976, congressional appropriations for Medicaid funding came attached with the so-called Hyde Amendment, which prohibits the use of federal funds in most abortions.[16] In effect, the Hyde Amendment meant that, in the words of sociologist Zakiya Luna, "a rich woman using private insurance and a poor woman using federal government insurance both have a legal right to an abortion, but only the first one can be assured she can obtain the abortion."[17]

The Hyde Amendment, however, contains a notable exception for cases of "life endangerment, rape or incest." In the eyes of the state, even these yet-to-be children are not meant to live. They are unlovable and unworthy. This observation is not to say anything about a woman's right to choose. I support my own mother's right to choose and think that aborting me would have saved her years of pain and trauma every time she looked at me. Instead, my point is that socioeconomic and political decisions that control access to resources are another way that we collectively demonstrate who is worthy of love.

This is the case even for so-called "good" and "progressive" movements like that of climate change advocates. For example, white climate change advocates from the Global North often link the fate of the environment to individual women's reproductive decisions. The ideal women, who environmental and gender scholar Jade Sasser describes as "sexual stewards," are "assumed to be fertile, reproducing beings, whose improved status will ideally lead to making responsible family choices— choices that include the *proper* spacing, timing, and number of children that will slow global population growth."[18] Sasser goes on to note that these "population-climate narratives tend to naturalize poverty and inequality in the Global South. In advocacy trainings, images of the poor are presented as dark-skinned women of color,

often in tattered clothing and surrounded by children…
these images…are…constructed representations, informed
by colonial legacies."[19] Constructions of worthiness, race,
gender, and resources go hand-in-hand and reproduce
what Du Bois refers to as a global color line.[20] But placing
the burden of climate change on individual women doesn't
have to be the case. Nonprofits and advocates like Colette
Pichon Battle at the Gulf Coast Center for Law and Policy,
to name one example, provide alternative solutions by
working in collaboration with local communities of color
to create sustainable economies based on organizational
values of human rights, restorative justice, equity, shared
liberation, and sovereignty and self-determination.[21] Solutions, in this vein, are structural and community-centered
practices, and not based on individual reproductive
decisions.

What, then, does it mean to see love as something used
by individuals, a bundle of practices, and as something that
is structural, unevenly distributed, and shapes decisions? It
means understanding love as working through organizations like governments, schools, and workplaces. Seeing it
in this way helps clarify that where we put our federal,
state, local, and personal resources is a matter of who and
what is loved and thus is seen as valuable and worthy.[22]

In the world of academia, love and worth starts with who
gets in. At both the undergraduate and graduate level,
admissions committees assess applications that contain
multiple moving parts, ranging from transcripts, SAT/ACT

scores, and GRE scores, to personal essays, research statements, and letters of recommendations. Admissions decisions are judgments of worth, based on students' application materials. But these judgments are not "objective." Each portion of the application bumps up against larger structural and social forces, mirroring societal feelings about who, what, and how someone is deemed worthy. For example, levels of school preparation and standardized scores are linked to school resources, which are themselves the product of racism regarding how space, place, and neighborhoods are organized.[23]

The nebulousness of admissions criteria is amplified at the graduate level, where departments are making decisions that effectively decide who will constitute their future profession.[24] For graduate students, admission is often contingent upon identifying a member of the faculty willing to mentor the applicant, which entails a great deal of time and investment into a person. So, when a faculty member agrees, that often reflects their willingness to work with someone and the potential they see in molding the applicant into a future valuable member of the profession.

Once admitted to a program, graduate students are subjected to a continual, and often public, assessment of their perceived worthiness, and many come to understand their place in the hierarchy through their relationship—or lack thereof—with their mentors. It's about *who* gets *what kind* of mentorship *from whom*. Mentorship, like the love of a parent, is not evenly distributed.

Not all graduate students get close attention from mentors, who decide where and how to split their time. Some mentors don't provide close mentorship to anyone, others may decide that some students are more worthy of attention than others. Some PhD candidates get regular meetings or line-by-line edits of their work, while others are left to sink or swim mostly on their own or with whatever help they cobble together from their peers and communities. Still others are groomed for sexual harassment. Mentors' time, attention, and care—their emotional capital—is then converted to other types of capital, such as social capital in the form of networks and job advocacy. It also is converted to publishing peer-reviewed publications—the expected output of academic labor, which provides access to jobs, funding, and awards—especially if the papers are published in journals considered to be among the most important in the field.

The types of resources faculty provide also depend on their own status and resources. Faculty who are required to teach more courses (particularly new courses), have multiple service demands, don't have resources like research funds and graduate research assistantships to help with their work, or don't have staff to help write grants and fellowships may not be able to provide their students with close attention because their time—our most precious resource—is stretched too thin. Academic "stars" at well-resourced universities, with few courses to teach, few service responsibilities, staff available to help with grant writing and teaching needs, and funds for their research can focus more on their own research and subsequent publications and may not want to invest their time in students.

Academia is also a workplace. People talk about "loving your work" or "finding a job you love" to emphasize the individualized feelings that people get when they take satisfaction from a job well done. But if we take seriously the idea of love as a bundle of practices, as a form of capital, and as shaping decisions, we must think about what we're saying when we use the language of affect to describe a labor relationship. Does your job love you? What does it mean when your coworkers, colleagues, audiences, or others love you, your work, or how you performed during a job interview? What shapes these processes? Lauren Rivera talks about elite investment, consulting, and law firms' practice of hiring based on what she calls "cultural matching," or how employers assess applicants who are culturally similar to themselves as better candidates than those who are culturally dissimilar.[25] In this sense, we can see how love is shorthand for recognition and affinity, and how "liking" something or someone is on the shallow end of the love scale. Our feelings about whom and what we love shape daily life, from whom we hang out with to what we do when we're together. Frequently, these emotions correlate to how similar we are to one another—what scholars term "homophily."[26] Similarity breeds like, love, and affinity. It marks who is worthy and who is not.

In the workplace of academia, hiring often comes down to "fit,"[27] that nebulous concept that is racialized, gendered, and sexualized.[28] Advice columns tell people on the academic job market that fit can range from whether candidates "get along" with departmental colleagues to whether or not they are perceived to be "eager" to be a part of their community or use the job as a "stepping stone" for another job down the road.[29] Through this idea and language of fit—which is often used as shorthand for whether faculty members like you want you to be their colleague, and respect your work and where it is published—love and worth shape who gets tenure-stream jobs and what work gets rewarded. Scholars' worthiness is continually assessed by peer reviewers and hiring, award, and grant committees. Once again, these evaluations of merit, quality, and significance are based on subjective criteria that reflect abstract feelings of love and worth.[30]

Academic life is built on rejections. Even the most successful faculty members have been rejected by jobs, journals, grants, and fellowships. But when you're an outsider, those rejections are just another in the long list of ways that you've been told that you're different, not good enough, and not worthy of care. The academic system rewards those with the emotional capital—and associated cultural and social capital—to understand and deal with rejections.

Some scholars come to the academy having been assured their whole lives (whether they realize it or not) that they are deserving and worthy. A bad peer review, or a failed job search, may be the first serious rejection they've encountered. While difficult, they move past it. Eventually. It's harder for the rest of us.

I remember my very first journal rejection. I was sitting in a crowded coffee shop in downtown DC when I opened up the review files. Tears rolled down my cheeks as I read the words that questioned whether the paper was even sociological. I forwarded the rejection to my mentor, and we quickly chatted on the phone about what the reviewers said and what I should do next. But I couldn't get past the report itself. Its words crushed me: What was sociological about my project? It seemed like an indictment of my very being. A judgment of my labor and thought, one that found my work lacking, not even recognizable as something worthy to be considered sociology.

Years later, I've learned to take harsh comments and translate them. To parse out the nuggets of useful information and concrete things I can do to make my argument stronger. To discard that which was a wholesale rejection of my very ideas. It's safe to say that being asked what was sociological about my paper is not the harshest comment I've ever received. But that first rejection, on a paper that I had worked two years on, devastated me because it questioned my worthiness to be a sociologist.

For outsiders—for those of us who doubt our ability to be loved—the kinds of rejections that structure academic life can foster imposter syndrome, the feeling that you're not good enough and don't belong. This endless cycle of evaluation and potential rejection feeds into a cycle of negativity or doubt precisely because society has told us we're unworthy our entire lives. Everyone experiences rejection, but our *experience* of these rejections is not the same.

On one hand, we have been told (and I am guilty of this too) to accept these rejections. To push through. It takes grit and a thick skin, we are told, to make it in academia. Peer review is rigorous, and the trade of academic work is ideas—we must sharpen them to make them useful and relevant. All of this is true.

On the other hand, it is also true that not everyone receives the same *type* of rejections. While in theory, peer review for journals is double-blind, meaning the author doesn't know who is reviewing the paper and vice versa, the field is small enough that it often is not double-blind. And bias is built into the peer review system, where critical scholarship, often produced by people of color, is seen as less rigorous, more "narrow," and not generalizable. Not good fits for the top journals in the field. In practice, people also often use peer review to push their scholarship and that of their friends—asking authors to cite these works—because of how valuable they perceive this scholarship and approach peer review through tearing down papers, especially those they do not agree with.

And it's not a secret whose work gets seen as rigorous, generalizable, and important and whose does not. It's predictable, quantifiable, and built into the foundations of academy. That is, faculty of color are the ones often pushed out and told they are not rigorous, whether in the peer-review system, hiring process, or in merit and promotion. Jane Junn and Ma'a K. Davis Cross,[31] for example, collected and analyzed data on tenure for faculty in the social sciences and humanities at the University of Southern California—difficult data to access across universities due to confidentiality rules—and found that between 1998 and 2012, 92% of white male faculty,[32] compared to 55.1% of all other faculty (white women, people of color), were awarded tenure and only 48% of faculty of color were tenured compared to 81% of white faculty, regardless of gender. They also found that during tenure processes, USC administrators violated stated procedures, ignored tenure standards, and breached hiring contracts.

But harsh, biased assessments of work don't have to be the way that peer review is run. Instead, my own writing groups and book workshops—often composed of women of color—provide an alternative, one where we read each other's works for their potential and contribution, offering ways to make the argument stronger. Sociologists Zakiya Luna and Whitney N. Laster Pirtle would describe this approach as part of the practice of Black Feminist Sociology which sees "love [as] consistent with the ethos of agape—a way of doing that seeks to minimize the load we carry and escalate kindness, grace, support, uplift, reflection and care."[33]

Too often, scholars invoke the idea of grit and self-discipline to explain who succeeds in school and who fails.[34] This language focuses on the individual who is rejected and not on the system of rejections that prioritizes the worth of certain types of people, backgrounds, experiences, scholarship, and writing over others. And yet we know that who gets love in academia—that is, who is welcomed within its walls, who gets jobs, awards, publications in top journals, citations, and the like—-is often, though not always, based on networks, status, and prestige.[35] Some of us will never receive these kinds of recognition. Others may achieve the coveted honors we desperately want. But, what then?

In 2019, I arrived at the National Women's Studies Association's annual meeting two days before it began to attend the Women of Color Leadership Project, a competitive preconference that mentors and supports women of color. I remember sitting around a set of tables, surrounded by Black, Brown, Indigenous, and otherwise marginalized scholars. We were talking about goals and visions for our careers.

I raised my hand to ask a question: How can we center *our* goals and visions if achieving them depends on others? I gave an example: if I wanted to publish in the flagship journal in my field, that isn't up to me. It's up to the editors and peer reviewers, and what they think of my work.

The workshop leader responded by challenging me to think about why I wanted to publish in a particular place—what would that accomplish?

That question shook me to the core. I'm certain it was not the first time someone asked me it. But it was the first time I was in a place to really hear it.

It would finally prove that I'm worthy, I replied, that I am accepted and good enough.

She responded: but even if you published there, some people would still think you're not good enough. And right now, here, there is a whole room of women who think you are good enough already.

I spent the next days, weeks, months finding myself drawn back to what she said. Maybe it was the almost two decades of therapy. Or having published my first book. Or having two kids. But the truth of her words stuck with me. I am good enough. Why do I need the elite of the academy to tell me that I'm worthy?

I find myself thinking, too, of a white lesbian scholar who, when I mentioned how my work cuts across multiple subfields, asked, "Who shows you the love?" She was asking me to see who already recognizes my value. By virtue of being here, there are already people in your corner. As I have progressed in my career, I've realized that there are people who do value me and my work. They just might not be at my own department.

I have devoted my life to chasing love, worth, and recognition in my profession in the hopes that it will fill the emptiness that comes from feeling unloved, unworthy. It doesn't. It hasn't. Instead, academic work often leaves me feeling not good enough, no matter how many accolades I receive. When I judge my CV against the professional "ideal" cemented in my head through grad school and professional socialization, I always fall short. I'm not at a top five, or even a top ten or top twenty-five graduate program in sociology. In fact, I'm not even in a sociology department anymore. I don't have publications in the top two journals in my field.

My book didn't win this award or that recognition. I didn't get this fellowship or that large grant. This way of thinking and measuring my worth will always and has always exhausted and depleted me. It will never replenish me.

It has taken me much longer than I care to admit to realize that I shouldn't be spending time on people who will inevitably dismiss me. And unfortunately, it's still something I continually struggle against. Love and worth in the academy are not about our worthiness, our ability to be loved, as individuals. They're based on structures that reject those for whom they weren't made. And yet, the profession is big, much bigger than the elite spaces that use the language and practices of love and worth to enforce existing hierarchies. I'm learning to seek out and amplify those spaces and advocates who appreciate scholars for who they are, no matter how prestigious their work.

Life is also much bigger than our professional commitments and our paid (and unpaid) labor. Life is full of joys and pleasure, both big and small, that replenish my sense of worth. My afternoon cup of chai at Crave, my kids' laughter, the delight on their faces when I pick them up from school, their hugs. The supernatural romance books I read with my grandma, my trips to the local bookstore owned by my friend, texts from friends, binging TV shows, finally buying the sweater or dress I've been eyeing, listening to my podcasts while I run: all of these things bring a smile to my face. Even and often when everything else around me seems to be on fire, they remind me that I, too, am worthy of love. We all are.

CONDITIONAL CITIZENSHIP

Dusk fell as I scrambled to say goodbye to my daughter and grandma. Rushing out the door, trying to balance carrying the food that I was bringing for the dinner with my purse, all while Olivia tugged at my leg, I headed out. It was just me, Olivia and my grandma. Like any parent of a toddler or young child, I hadn't been sleeping much. I felt frazzled wherever I went. Especially when I was in a rush. Which felt like always.

I drove up to the house, nestled into the woods, and paused to catch my breath before stepping out of my car. I was eager to make a good impression, but also anxious because I didn't know what to expect. I knocked on the door. The host opened it, welcoming me in. I entered the kitchen, where everyone gathered. Everyone else was a white woman, all faculty except for one postdoc. I stood awkwardly next to the kitchen island. I picked at the appetizers and drank a cup of white wine, listening in on the small talk, and nodding my head to signal I was following along.

A famous white woman professor introduced herself and mentioned one of my graduate school mentors. It had only been a few minutes since I arrived. Still frazzled, I was thinking about my daughter's crying. Would I leave her in Grandma's room when I returned home, or bring her into mine? When this woman mentioned my mentor, my mind immediately went to my mentor's kindness and generosity. I launched into a brief story about how, when I had a miscarriage during fieldwork, my mentor was so thoughtful and considerate. As the words left my mouth, I noticed a shift in this person's face.

Immediately, I knew I failed a test. That person, and the other women in the kitchen, didn't care about my personal life or how wonderful a person my mentor was. They weren't there to talk about emotions. I quickly followed up with how one of my mentor's books was transformative. The white woman professor smiled, nodded her head, and agreed. Then she turned away. I felt dismissed: judged and found not worthy of that person's time or even polite conversation.

Fuck, I thought to myself. I knew better. Why did I lead with the personal? I was so tired, but I knew I needed to step up my game. I desperately wanted to impress these women. I vowed to do better. But as I turned to listen to the broader conversation, all that I heard were conversations that confirmed my worst fears that I wasn't good enough.

Everyone was gossiping about job placement: who got a job where and why, and who failed to get one. This is the academic draft, where job placement represents the pinnacle of love and worth, of who belongs and who is worthy of entering the esteemed ranks of the professoriate. And, conversely, who doesn't. Of course, the discussion centered on the top five, sometimes top ten, or occasionally the top twenty-five grad programs. There I was, the only woman of color in the room. I was from an immigrant family and worked at a liberal arts college. I felt invisible.

In some senses, I was, and am, immensely privileged. Here I was, "lucky" enough to be invited to this gathering, to be there, in this room among the elite of the elite. But I could tell I was a no one. I was an outsider within[1]: allowed to listen in on the conversation and hear the behind-the-scenes gossip, but not invited as a full citizen of the group. No one there cared about my thoughts on that topic or any other. I felt worthless and out of place.

I stayed at the potluck a few more minutes—maybe a half hour in all, making an excuse about needing to get back to my daughter and grandma. I hurried and left. Defeated. Distracted with thoughts of my daughter, I had briefly forgotten that every encounter was a test I needed to pass. I have to prove my worth and value every time I met new people and changed roles, institutions, and stages in my career. To be an outsider, a racialized outsider, is to be uncomfortable. It means never letting your guard down, especially with people whom you do not completely trust. And it's hard to know whom to trust.

Being excluded in the academy is as an active and ongoing process, not a one-time event. It is not (solely) due to lack of information, knowledge, or cultural capital about the "hidden curriculum." Certainly, it helps to know the rules of the game. But the active exclusion of racialized and gendered outsiders is more systemic than this, structuring all aspects of academic life, from our interactions with others, to the courses we take (for students), the materials we teach, and the system of rewards that punctuate careers.[2] This form of active exclusion means that marginalized outsiders are denied *academic citizenship*, that is, the legal rights and responsibilities of, as well as full acceptance and inclusion into, academic life. Full citizenship means having your voice valued, sought out, heard, and respected in decision-making processes. For marginalized outsiders, academic citizenship is conditional.

When sociologists speak of "citizenship" in the national context, they are generally referring not only to legal status, but also to belonging, political participation, and sets of practices and claims-making related to upholding and investing in the nation-state.[3] In thinking about academic citizenship, I am drawing on work in the social sciences and humanities on "cultural citizenship."[4] Aihwa Ong, for example, argues that cultural citizenship consists of the cultural practices and beliefs that shape the relationship between the state and its people, that is, "becoming a citizen depends on how one is constituted as a subject who exercises or submits to power relations."[5] More recently, sociologist Jean Beaman uses this framework to unpack how France's ongoing racial and colonial projects deny the French children of North African immigrants cultural citizenship, despite the fact that they are legal citizens.[6]

In a similar vein, Laila Lalami uses the term *conditional citizenship* to describe her relationship to the state and people like her "whose rights the state finds expendable in the pursuit of white supremacy."[7] The same kinds of conditional inclusion can be found in academic life.

I use the more general term *academic citizenship* since I see legal, institutional, cultural, and political forms of membership as entwined, unable to be disentangled from one another. Academic citizenship concerns not only the rights and responsibilities of those in the academy, which are differentiated and tied to rank, whether that be graduate student, postdoc, adjunct, tenure-line, or tenured faculty. It also encompasses the sense of belonging, access to political participation, and sets of practices and claims-making related to academic life, all of which are racialized, gendered, and classed. Service labor is frequently considered part of being a good academic citizen[8] and is similarly racialized, gendered, and classed. But instead of focusing on the *responsibilities* of faculty citizenship, my focus here is on the *rights* associated with that role. That is, who has full access to those rights, and who does not?

What does conditional academic citizenship look like in practice? Exclusion vis-à-vis patterned interactions is extensively documented.[9] In a 2020 viral Twitter hashtag #BlackintheIvory created by Shardé Davis and popularized by Joy Melody Woods,[10] for example, Black scholars shared their experiences of racism, sexism, and misogynoir in the academy.[11] These experiences include, but are not limited to, racial microaggressions,"[12] though Ibram X. Kendi prefers the term "racist abuse" because "abuse accurately describes the action and its effects on people: distress, anger, worry, depression, anxiety, pain, fatigue, and suicide."[13] These interactions are constant reminders of who belongs and who doesn't, of who is able to be a full participant in academic life and whose presence and acceptance is conditional. They can take the form of off-handed comments that are likely soon forgotten by the people who make them, but which have lasting influence on those who receive them.

Let's take graduate students' informal encounters with faculty and fellow graduate students as an example. I remember one such conversation with a faculty member I liked and respected—and whom I continue to like and respect—early on in my graduate career. We were walking down a hall and talking about Philippe Bourgois's *In Search of Respect*. I had recently read it and mentioned how evocative his writing was, that it brought me inside the story. They replied something to the effect of, oh yeah, like you've smoked crack or been to a crack house, a passing and dismissive comment that was seeped in racialized anti-Black assumptions about who smokes crack and who does not. The comment stopped me in my tracks. I had, in fact, experimented with drugs, including hard ones like acid and crack, though that seems a lifetime ago.

I remember bits and pieces of the one and only time I smoked crack. I was fourteen years old. Just a few months earlier, I had had my worst fears about my father confirmed. That devastating news sent me on to what would thankfully be a relatively short detour onto a path that might have ended with me in jail, dead, or worse. I dropped previous friends and started hanging out with the so-called "druggies" at the school. But it didn't stop there.

There was the time I was in the backseat of the car, while the man that I lost my virginity to—and I do mean man, he was twenty-three and I was fourteen—and a friend of his were in the front seats. I started to feel heavy, was unable to really move or talk. I suspected that my weed was laced with something other than what I'd tried before.

The night I tried acid, my friend and I snuck out of her house in the middle of the night. We went over to my apartment complex, to an apartment where a group of guys lived and whom we had befriended. One had a sheet of acid and offered me a hit. I sat on the couch, seeing colors in my mind's eye for the first time in my life. Time stopped. Or sped up. I blacked out and don't remember anything. The next thing I know, people are flushing the drugs down the toilet and I'm being ushered outside by the police. My grandma and her boyfriend are waiting there. They had found out we were there because my friend's mom called the cops when she didn't find us in my friend's bedroom.

The first and only time I tried crack I remember being in a small, dark, and cramped room. The twenty-something man I was with had a pipe in his hands, put a rock in, and flicked on his lighter. He passed it to me. I don't remember what I was thinking or feeling at the time. I suspect I was nervous and wanted to just not feel that pit of darkness that resided deep within me.

These are the types of experiences that are seen as a goldmine for ethnographers and qualitative scholars, especially those who study poverty or crime. But they aren't (supposed to be) the experiences of someone who shows up in academic hallways and at conferences, writing papers, or at academic social gatherings. If a scholar has had similar experiences, they typically only reveal it—and selectively at that—if they study people in similar situations. And we don't share our experiences of racist or gendered abuse because we're constantly being told that we misinterpreted (patterned) interactions.

Dismissive and offhand comments and microaggressions foster fears of not being taken seriously, all of which are forms of silencing. Academic outsiders are silenced in myriad ways, unable or unwilling to share parts of themselves and their experiences because of how different we are from people with the kinds of middle- and upper-class white backgrounds that produce academia's ideal worker.[14]

In that moment, and in many moments throughout my career, I was reminded of where I was. What was acceptable and what was not. Who belonged and who did not. Whose family backgrounds counted and whose couldn't be spoken about. I also couldn't or can't talk about close family members being in and out of jail, whether for drugs, kidnapping, or dog fighting. Or about how, growing up, my grandma spent money I had given her to save so that I could buy a car. She didn't tell me until I started looking at cars to purchase months later. Or about that time when I was in college that my uncle forged my IRS refund check. I am also unlikely to share stories from my wedding, where people left the backyard reception, only to return with hard liquor. A family member-in-law called my uncle a "Filipino pussy" and threw liquor in his face. What I remember most is him seething in rage, holding my head in both his hands, telling me how he didn't hurt her because of me. Even now, I am hesitant talk in academic settings about my uncle's recent death and how the police refused to let paramedics enter his son's apartment after he collapsed, despite his son pleading with the police to let them go in.

Back to that moment, in that hallway, I was reminded that my presence there was conditional, based on my silence.

And what does it mean for me to be breaking that silence now, to be sharing these private experiences in a book published by an academic press? It means I'm tired. Exhausted by the constant labor of managing a presentation of self that is stripped down, devoid of any remnants of who I am or how I grew up.

In the academic workplace, especially in elite spaces, the model background is far from my own. Any mention of any part of my life can immediately shut down conversation or evoke pity. But I just want to be recognized and treated as fully human, a valued member of the academy, not as someone to be pitied or exalted. To just exist.

Within scholarly disciplines, the "canon" of a given field, what is read, cited, learned, and taught, also establishes the boundaries of conditional citizenship. Indeed, in 1994 Renato Rosaldo explicitly wrote and theorized about cultural citizenship in the context of democratizing education through an inclusive curriculum that reflects the varied histories and materials of the changing demographics of students and the world we live in.[15] Twenty years later, Aldon Morris's *The Scholar Denied* was a wake-up call for many sociologists to reckon with our own discipline's racist foundations, including the erasure of W.E.B. Du Bois and the Atlanta School from our origin story.[16] The publication of Morris's book brought into mainstream sociology long-standing, but largely ignored, critiques of the politics of citation and the "canon."[17] It also spurred similar research.[18] The viral hashtag and movement #CiteBlackWomen similarly brought to the foreground the systemic erasure of Black women and their writings in the production of knowledge,[19] as did sociologist Adia Harvey Wingfield's call to similarly situate Black women's experiences and contributions to academia.[20]

I used to teach classical sociological theory for undergraduates. Traditionally, the syllabus for this course focuses on the work of old white[21] men. The list can include Herbert Spencer and Auguste Comte, who both promoted the use of science to justify racism. That's not how I taught it. In my classical theory course, I taught Black scholars such as Ida B. Wells-Barnett, W.E.B. Du Bois, and Anna Julia Cooper, as well as white women scholars like Jane Addams. Over and over again, whether in class, in private meetings, over email, or in student evaluations, my students express surprise, gratitude, and excitement for reading the works of scholars of color and seeing how applicable their writings are to today. More than one student stated how they never knew before this class that there were women theorists.

Centering scholars of color and their writings is not the norm in classical theory or even in most sociology courses, even after the publication of *The Scholar Denied* and recent mass mobilizations against anti-Black racism. Sociology, as a discipline, continues to resist calls to decenter white scholars, despite calls for more inclusion from both students and faculty.

The conditionality of academic citizenship also occurs in how bureaucratic policies are practiced and implemented: what law and society scholars refer to as "law in action." For example, the University of California system includes a policy called Bylaw 55, which dictates who in the department holds voting rights on decisions regarding hiring, merits, and promotions. Bylaw 55 grants tenured faculty the right to vote on whether to extend voting rights to assistant professors. That is, associate and full professors vote on whether assistant professors can vote on hiring other assistant professors, associate professors, and full professors (three different votes). Another section of Bylaw 55 establishes similar voting rights for decisions on merit and promotion of other assistant professors, associate professors, and full professors. Yet another provision allows full professors to vote on whether to extend voting rights to associate professors, that is, whether associate professors can vote on hiring and promotion of full professors. Every department on every UC campus must vote on these policies each year.[22]

These votes may be passive or affirmative. For example, in a well-functioning department that takes an affirmative approach, each year the department chair asks the faculty whether they want to retain the same voting eligibility as the previous year. This decision requires little to no discussion or time in the first faculty meeting of the year, when the vote is required to be taken. Other well-functioning departments take a more passive approach, only bringing Bylaw 55 up for discussion when someone requests that the votes be revisited.

In inclusive departments, all faculty get all rights; all faculty are full citizens in the department. Other departments may assign rights to each rank. For example, assistants may be permitted to vote on hiring at any rank but may not be able to participate in the merit and promotion decisions of any of their colleagues. For the purpose of this discussion, what matters is that, within these departments, these rights and responsibilities remain consistent from year to year. In dysfunctional and toxic departments, however, Bylaw 55 is weaponized to further divide who belongs and who doesn't.

This is exactly what happened in my former department. Many years ago—or so I'm told—full voting rights were extended to everyone. Then it changed, so that voting rights were not extended to any assistant professors. I think, but am unsure, that change occurred the year that the assistant professors were two white women and one women of color. After that, the white women were promoted with tenure. That left the sole woman of color in the department the only assistant professor, who was stripped of voting rights. Once I arrived on campus, I encountered a system in which voting rights were constantly debated and seemingly changed depending on the whims of the senior white faculty. One year, we assistant professors were granted rights to vote on two separate hires at the assistant level, but not at the associate level. The department hired two excellent assistant professors of color. The next year, voting rights were again "not extended" on an associate-level hire, our only hire that year. The following year, we were granted full voting rights. But we were not hiring.

Yet even though we were excluded from the final decision-making process, assistant professors were asked to do the invisible labor associated with hiring and promotion. We served on the recruitment committee, contributed to senior colleagues' files for merit and promotion, and served as lead reviewers for the files of tenured colleagues, providing in-depth assessments of a colleague's research, teaching, and service. This was in addition to the countless hours we spent mired in the details of the hiring process itself: participating in faculty meetings, reading applicants' files, attending job talks and dinners, and being drawn into (at times, lengthy) informal discussions about candidates. All of this without the benefits of full departmental citizenship; all of this with our citizenship status contested and fluctuating each year.

That year and the next, I and others spent hours trying to convince senior faculty of the value of "giving" us rights. It was exhausting. Two assistant professors of color left the department. Another year, after being asked to attend the department meeting by another assistant professor even though I was on leave, I sent an email describing what was at stake in limiting assistant professors' departmental citizenship. Of course, assistant professors weren't the only faculty without rights. So were our lecturers. I once asked someone to include our lecturers on our department website, because at that time they weren't even deemed worthy enough of being listed. The response I received was that they had to first double-check.

In the email I tried to be as diplomatic as possible.

I explained that voting rights are important because they denote full citizenship in the department. It matters who is given voting rights. I furthered stated that, if rights weren't extended, I would no longer be able to do the service work connected to decisions in which I had been barred from participating. Instead, I would focus on my research to better align my time to the tenure expectations of an assistant professor at an R1 university.

The response was about what I had expected. Although I received individual emails thanking me for the email, I also received an email accusing me of threatening to withdraw my labor (rather than—as I saw it—aligning my labor with my rights). The response continued by telling me that I was wrong to imply that the current policy was racist and sexist. They explained that assistant professors of color had been given voting rights in the past, albeit when the majority of assistant professors were white. Therefore, this person said, it wasn't and couldn't be racist that assistant professors (all of whom were of color) weren't currently given voting rights.

In requesting and being denied respect—whether that be full citizenship rights or the ability to align our time and labor with our rights—faculty who are from marginalized groups often face institutional betrayals. As Carly Parnitzke Smith and Jennifer J. Freyd define the term, an institutional betrayal "occurs when an institution causes harm to an individual who trusts or depends upon that institution."[23] I was specifically recruited to University of California, Riverside as a Target of Excellence hire and was excited to accept the offer. But I felt betrayed when we (myself and my fellow assistant professors) weren't even considered worthy of voting rights. This and similar types of betrayals are part and parcel of what constitutes conditional academic citizenship.

University hiring, merit, and promotion systems, with their emphasis on the "quality" of someone's research, are designed to reproduce conditional citizenship. Which journals a person publishes in, where they received their PhD, who wrote their letters of recommendation—all have a status hierarchy. Access to these status markers are themselves the product of who gets the benefit of the doubt on whether they can "succeed"—that is, an editor has to decide whether a person will be able to successfully revise a paper; a graduate admissions committee has to decide whether a person will fit into and do well in a graduate program. Decisions on hiring, merit, and promotion include how many publications a person has as well as any awards, fellowships, and grants. These decisions can make or break people's careers, especially for those whose papers, for example, are on the "borderline" of being given a revise and resubmit versus a rejection from a journal. They come down to who is shown love and worth in the academy and the racialized politics behind what constitutes merit.[24]

Practices that deny full academic citizenship are often built into the evaluations of teaching and service. Women and men faculty of color, queer faculty, queer faculty of color, white women, and others are subject to biased student evaluations of teaching,[25] called upon to do more (undervalued) service work, and are less likely to hold positions of power. Much of service work consists of what Wingfield and Alston call "racialized tasks," or "the work minorities do that is associated with their position in the organizational hierarchy and reinforces Whites' position of power in the workplace."[26] Scholars of color, particularly junior scholars like grad students, postdocs, assistant professors, and precarious workers like adjuncts and lecturers, must additionally maintain a "professional" presentation of self in their classes and in interactions with colleagues. This is, Wingfield and Alston write, because "not only the demographics but the culture of academia is distinctly white, heterosexual, and middle- and upper-middle-class. Those who differ from this norm find themselves, to a greater or lesser degree, 'presumed incompetent' by students, colleagues, and administrators."[27] So while everyone has a professional presentation of self, scholars of color are that much more pressured to fit into the norm of an "ideal worker" that doesn't fit our lives, commitments, or experiences.

Despite, or perhaps because of, this extra labor scholars of color are often pushed out of traditional disciplinary departments, forced through bullying, harassment, and hostile work environments to make "critical exits" to interdisciplinary departments. Some leave academia altogether.[28] I count myself among the former group. The tenure process is particularly embattled, as shown by the many narratives documented in the volume *Written/Unwritten: Diversity and the Hidden Truths of Tenure*, edited by Patricia Matthews. This result is, as Patricia Hill Collins writes, "neither accidental nor benign. Suppressing the knowledge produced by any oppressed group makes it easier for dominant groups to rule because the seeming absence of dissent suggests that subordinate groups willingly collaborate in their own victimization."[29]

Even diversity officers—the very people hired "to institutionalize diversity"[30]—are met with everyday acts and experiences of resistance. Too often and at too many institutions, their very presence becomes the ends (a sign of progress) rather than the means (a way to address the racism, stereotypes, resistance, and other obstacles people of color face) for equity and inclusion in the academy. As Sara Ahmed notes, raising problems becomes translated into being the problem.[31]

Universities are examples of what Victor Ray calls "racialized organizations," which "are meso-level racial structures" that connect racial ideologies with material resources.[32] In doing do, Ray writes, they "expand or inhibit agency, legitimate the unequal distribution of resources, treat Whiteness as a credential, and decouple organizational procedures in ways that typically advantage dominant racial groups."[33] Universities are also what Joan Acker calls "gendered organizations," which "means that advantage and disadvantage, exploitation and control, action and emotion, meaning and identity, are patterned through and in terms of a distinction between male and female, masculine and feminine. Gender is not an addition to ongoing processes . . . Rather, it is an integral part of those processes."[34] In this sense, organizations like universities institutionalize multiple interlocking systems of oppression,[35] and they do so through what Acker calls inequality regimes, those "loosely interrelated practices, processes, actions, and meanings that result in and maintain class, gender, and racial inequalities."[36]

These same gendered, sexualized, and racialized practices, meanings, and processes also occur in specific disciplines—like sociology, the discipline I am in—as well as the profession more generally. Academic disciplines are fields of power, where people enact constant conflict and cooperation over symbolic and material goods, services, and resources that increase status, opportunities, and prestige.[37] Entry into this field in not neutral nor completely based on merit. Merit does matter. But privilege and whiteness—separately or combined—matter just as much or even more and cannot be separated from merit.[38]

Being an academic outsider is a problem that is seemingly intractable. That's because everything is stacked against us. Although the number of faculty of color may be increasing, it is increasing at the level of adjuncts and lecturers.[39] Within institutions, faculty of color are often concentrated within interdisciplinary departments, which tend to receive less resources and support than disciplinary departments. Power in the academic workplace—whether that be at the elite PhD departments and institutions whose graduates make up the bulk of people getting tenure-stream jobs or leadership positions within particular universities—remains concentrated in the hands of white, cis, heterosexual men and, to a lesser extent, white, cis, heterosexual women. The same goes for journal editorships.

This power that stops academic outsiders in their tracks is maintained through tokenism, a phenomenon in which one person or only a handful of people from marginalized communities are asked to stand in for a larger community in any given workplace or setting. The status quo is maintained through what Nancy Leong[40] calls "identity capitalism," by which she means the process through which members of an ingroup (in the US, most commonly white, cis, heterosexual men) use the identity of members of an outgroup (in the US, anyone who is nonwhite or nonheterosexual) for their own benefit.

In academia, knowledge that stems from personal experience is discounted, as is knowledge produced by people of color more generally. But when those same insights are written by white people about people of color, they are seen as innovative. That's because research on marginalized groups by faculty who belong to marginalized groups is often seen as suspect. The scholar's methods, substantive content, and theoretical orientations are dismissed as "me-search" or somehow "other," neither mainstream nor meeting the requirements of some sort of "scientific standard." It's not "rigorous" or "objective" enough. This type of work is rarely published in the "top" journals of a given discipline.[41] Instead, marginalized scholars' work is seen as "advocacy" or part of "identity politics" rather than "scholarship," as if what someone studies isn't linked to their backgrounds and interests.[42]

These debates about what constitutes "science," including the role of bias, date back to the beginnings of our discipline.[43] They form the basis of academic power.[44] But focusing on questions of individual "identity" ignores the structures of power that systematically disenfranchise, silence, and exclude outsiders. It ignores the interlocking systems of oppression—gendered racism, queerphobia, and so many others—that erect barriers and enact harm. It moves attention away from what Christine Williams calls organizational gaslighting, or what happens when organizations "intentionally deny the facts and blame others for the problems they generate. [They] attempt to puff up their own image while denying evidence of their malfeasance, enabling them to escape culpability for the systemic inequalities they produce."[45] This focus on individual identity, then, shifts focus to specific individuals and their actions, not the broader systems which shape how we live and work.[46] Until the very foundations of academia are shattered and recreated, outsiders will never be granted full citizenship. Our citizenship will remain conditional.

My back went out for the first time while I was giving my daughter a hug. I was dropping her off at daycare. When I bent over, the pain in my back was unbearable. I dropped to the floor, frozen in place. Any movement caused more pain. I started crying. I couldn't handle the pain on top of everything else. My daughter's teacher appeared by my side, urging me to let her call an ambulance. I refused. I needed to go back home, pick up my grandma, and drive her to LAX. She was headed back to Cincinnati to be with my mother, who was in the middle of what would turn out to be a month-long stay in a hospital that ended in her dying from stage IV breast cancer, just months after her initial diagnosis.

Only a few weeks earlier, I had found out that my still-in-utero son's heart had abnormalities, holes where they shouldn't be. The doctors detected this during my third trimester. At thirty-five years old, my pregnancy was considered "geriatric," which meant that I was subject to more tests and surveillance. Even so, I was told that we wouldn't know the severity of his condition until he was born.

Pain radiated from my back as minutes went by. Parents of Olivia's daycare friends came and went, dropping off their children for the day and eyeing what was happening. When I was eventually able to move, I refused additional offers of care from Olivia's teacher. I managed to get in my car, pick up grandma, and take her to the airport as planned. I had no choice. No one else could do it. There were just the three of us in my little world: me, Grandma, and my daughter. And now, with Grandma in Cincinnati to be with my mom, it was just pregnant me and my daughter.

I was sitting at the desk in my office when I got the call that my mom died. I had already purchased a plane ticket to see her—I was literally leaving the next day. I sank out of my chair and onto the floor, crying.

After my mom's funeral, when Grandma, my daughter, and I returned home, our grief was palpable, pouring out of us. And yet the pain did not stop. Just a few months after the one-year anniversary of my mom's death, my grandma had a heart attack. I was lying in bed, reading my phone as I waited for my daughter to fall asleep. From her room Grandma called my name. I got up, opened my door, and went to her. She told me she thought she was having a heart attack. The rest is a blur. I rush to get the kids ready. I drive her to the hospital. She had asked me to call an ambulance; I don't know why I insist on driving.

Probably my nerves, anxiety and worries. By the time we arrive at the crowded ER, it's past midnight.

My grandma is eventually taken to the back, alone. I wait in the lobby with my kids. The hospital allowed only one visitor at a time, and I couldn't leave my kids alone. Eventually, I asked how long it would take and whether she would be admitted to the hospital. When the staff person told me it would be a while, we arranged to have them call me to let me know whether she was being admitted or whether I should come to pick her up. I gather up my sleepy and cranky kids. I try, and fail, to hold back tears as I drive back home. It was six months before the COVID shutdowns in March 2020.

A few hours later, I get a call that my grandma was being admitted. The next day, after I call multiple times, she is eventually given a room. When I bring my kids to the hospital, I am told that I cannot bring them up to see her: children are not allowed on her floor. I don't know what to do, who to call. I have no other family here. At a loss for what to do, I text another assistant professor in my department. She quickly agrees to come but tells me that she has to catch an Uber—she doesn't have a car. Only after she arrives to watch my two kids can I finally go up to see my grandma. I have never before thought of my grandma as fragile or frail. But those are the words that come to me as she sits in the hospital bed. I start to cry.

For the rest of the week, I relied on a few department colleagues who graciously agreed to watch my kids for an hour or two while I went to visit my grandma in the hospital. Back at the house, it was just me and my kids. For everything. Nap time. Bedtime. Bath time. Waking up. Meals. Picking up and dropping off Olivia to and from school. Homework. And with my grandma not there to watch my son, he was with me all day. Meanwhile, I tried to continue to write, teach my courses, mentor students, and do service work.

Before her heart attack, my grandma was my rock. She was someone I could rely on and whom I couldn't be without—she cooked, cleaned, and helped with the kids. With her, I wasn't outnumbered.

But even when she returned, it wasn't the same. It couldn't be. She wasn't the same. Our lives were once again scrambled, in need of being put back together. Somehow. Grandma now had eating restrictions and had been told to stop smoking. Told to stop drinking Mountain Dew. She was exhausted, had little energy or breath, and couldn't take the long walks she loved. There were more medical appointments and medications that neither of us could pronounce. I registered my son for daycare since Grandma could no longer keep up with him. With my job, neither could I. A few weeks later, she was hospitalized again, this time for pancreatitis. Cue more doctors and tests, more changes to her diet and medications.

More and more of my time was going into home, into caring for both my grandma and my kids. The increased responsibilities of my "second shift"[1] necessarily meant less time for and at work. I could barely keep up with the classes I was teaching, much less continue to write or apply for grants, fellowships, jobs, or the like. But I did try to write, if not daily, then at least regularly. I had to. In the back of my mind, I kept hearing the conversations I'd overhead throughout the years. About who was worthy and who was not. How people with children were talked about—as not being serious enough or not being committed enough to their research. I heard the constant admonishments of advice columnists about prioritizing writing no matter what, particularly if you are at a research university—the de facto implication being that if you aren't writing even when your world is collapsing, you won't succeed. And if you don't succeed, it'll be your own fault because you couldn't manage your time wisely.

It was during this time of self-doubt that I also saw, more clearly, how those who were white and in more privileged positions than mine could get leeway for family circumstances if they were already on the tenure track. They would be given the benefit of the doubt, even if there were delays in having their books published or large gaps of time in between articles. But that same leeway is not usually extended to scholars who are marginalized. Certainly not to grad students trying to find a job, or for tenure track faculty trying to find a different job. Any slowdown in research output for outsiders is a barrier to getting a job, holding onto one, or trying to move to a more resource-rich university. I stretched myself thin trying to juggle my paid employment with my unpaid care work.[2]

I'm lucky and privileged to have my grandma. We help and lean on one another. I have also felt the extra burden of care work every single day of the past several years, ever since I had my daughter and, especially a few years later, after I had my son. And my labor does not stop with their care, or even with the additional care work associated with managing my grandma's health. I find myself buried in paid labor, which is necessary to stave off financial precarity, to shelter my family from the weight of ever-growing bills and expenses and because of the ever-looming stress of being on the tenure track. I am not alone.

Sociologist Caitlyn Collins describes the "lifeworlds of motherhood" as "the distinctive social universe of individual experiences, interactions, organizations, and institutions shaping the employment and child-rearing possibilities that women can envision for themselves."[3] My lifeworld of motherhood, similar to that of many academic mothers, feels small and restrictive.[4] I learned early on that I needed to depend on myself, that I couldn't really trust anyone, that the collective policies and broader cultural schemas and understandings of what it means to be a mother in academia were stacked against me because they are marked by individualism. It was my choice to have children; therefore, motherhood was a burden I must carry.

On paper at least, the flexibility and faculty autonomy associated with the academic workplace would seem to be made for parents, particularly mothers. And to some extent, it is. I can leave work at almost any time to attend to my children's healthcare visits, parent-teacher conferences, and (pre-COVID) extracurricular activities like Olivia's soccer practice or karate classes. I can also leave work to take my grandmother to her healthcare appointments and to run necessary household errands. Not having a traditional nine-to-five job affords me these privileges. And yet, in practice, this intense flexibility often results in nonstop work. Especially as someone without the job security that tenure affords.

The work of a faculty member is manifold. This work involves teaching, research, service, mentoring, managing a budget, all alongside department and university politics, and many other things I'm sure I forgot to include. These never-ending responsibilities in fact mean that I am constantly and consistently working. All the time. Just to keep up on my ever-expanding to-do list. After my first book was published, I felt slightly less pressure to always be "on." But only slightly. The neoliberal logics of university life mean that we are always expected to do more. The work never ends.

Academia, like many high-pressure, elite professions, is demanding. So are children and motherhood responsibilities. Mary Blair-Loy identifies two common cultural schemas, or "institutionalized and partially internalized models for cognition, morality and emotion…[that] constrain and enable behavior"[5] that shape working professional mothers' lives. The first, what she calls "work devotion," demands 24/7 attention to work. This model was built around the ideal worker as a white, middle-class, married man, whose masculinity was predicated on his career. The second, what she calls "family devotion," centers on the intensive responsibilities of childcare and housework. This schema is based on the model of the white, middle-class, married woman who stays at home. Today's working professional mothers feel the contradictions inherent in these competing schemas, neither one of which reflects their lived experience. Especially as someone who is solo-parenting and providing for my family, I constantly feel the pull and tension of both.

The unpredictable and often overwhelming amount of care responsibilities that come with mothering result in what Shelley Correll, Stephen Benard, and In Paik call the "motherhood penalty."[6] By this, the authors mean how mothers—but not fathers—are rated and perceived more poorly than nonmothers in hiring decisions. Nor is motherhood safe to pursue once a person has been hired. Joan Williams uses the term "maternal wall" to refer to how mothers fail to fit the mold of managers' expectations of "ideal workers"—who they are, what they look like, and how they behave—and thus are pushed out of their careers. She also identifies practices that make it more likely that women opt out of the workforce "by their 'own choice,'" such as the never-ending demands of an executive schedule, how people bar advancement opportunities of anyone who expresses interest—even temporarily due to childcare—in part-time work, and the expectation that people who aim for top positions in their organization will relocate their lives and families anywhere for their work.[7] The very practices and cultural assumptions that underly how we think about work, including academic work, excludes mothers.[8]

Nor is motherhood, even academic motherhood, equal. It is marked by race. Shaped by class. Molded by migration status. Deeply contoured by the presence or absence of a co-parent living in the same city,[9] among so many other factors. As sociologist Dawn Dow argues in her book about Black middle-class mothers, race, class, and gender have "a persistent and continuous impact on these mothers' everyday experiences, decision-making and parenting practices."[10] The privilege of whiteness in society is in the taken-for-grantedness of not "having" to talk about race, or think about whether or not your child will be the only white child in school, in their friendship circle, or in extracurricular activities. Black mothers don't have a choice. They are faced, on a daily basis, with this additional labor because of the gendered anti-Black racism they and their loved ones experience.

I have gained that elusive thing in the academy: a tenure-track position. Still, the fact that I am an untenured mother of color means that I am living a life of precarity—financially, professionally, emotionally, and intellectually—for myself and for my children.

I was about four to five months pregnant with my daughter when I went on two campus interviews during my first foray into the job market. I don't remember if someone explicitly told me to, or whether I picked it up hearing horror stories in graduate school, but I did not mention my pregnancy. That was in keeping with the common advice, which is that, if you could help it and weren't showing, you don't say a word. Luckily, I wasn't yet showing. My first interview was a disaster. I had pregnancy brain, or "brain fog," and wasn't thinking clearly. I remember standing in front of the room and spilling my water all over the place, even before I started speaking. I couldn't formulate my thoughts around questions people asked. My second interview went a little better. But I remember going to the bathroom, nauseous, and trying to keep myself together.

I got a call extending an offer from the second place that I interviewed. Only after the offer was extended did I mention my pregnancy and the possibility of a delayed start date. The shock and immediate silence that followed was deafening. In fact, the chair of the department called back soon after, apologizing for his response and saying how excited he was for me to join the department. But after I started, this same person made remarks about not hiring a person for a visiting position because of possible childcare issues. Two tenured women faculty left the department shortly thereafter. I began to feel quite sure that I wouldn't have been hired if my pregnancy was known. The realization left me feeling angry and defeated.

During this time, I commuted to my job by train. My hours-long commute home regularly involved me crying in anger and frustration about my job. I always planned to use that time for writing and research, since I had an infant daughter at home and my campus hours were filled with students, service, courses, and course prep. But those plans increasingly went out the window because in my anger and frustration, I couldn't concentrate on my writing.

By the time I was pregnant with my son, I was in a somewhat more solid place in a new job. Technically, I started this job a year before I moved to campus, but I was officially on leave to allow me to conduct research through a postdoctoral fellowship. The arrangement allowed me to qualify for FMLA and other parental benefits in the University of California system. I remember feeling like I had to make sure I knew the policies inside and out: what I was entitled to and what I wanted. When I had a meeting with the department co-chairs to ask for release from two courses, I came armed with knowledge of the associated policies I was drawing on. It went smoothly, likely because I was prepared. But a truly just system wouldn't rely on individual faculty's ability to navigate a sea of bureaucracy. It would have structures in place and leadership to help support its members of the community. At some institutions, faculty unions fill this need.

Some institutions have also introduced policies that are supposed to mitigate the professional costs of care work. Yet too often these very structures reproduce the same inequities they claim to address. Stop-the-clock policies, for example, allow people to take an additional year before going up for tenure, and that "extra" year is not supposed to be negatively considered in how that faculty member is evaluated. But in practice, I've heard people reference the number of articles a person has published since their PhD, which can penalize people who've had children or other caregiving responsibilities since their record doesn't reflect the number of years they've had to fully concentrate on their work. That is, when faculty and administrators evaluate the record of scholars who have used these policies, they see the absence of output rather than the products of care. I worked through both pregnancies. Indeed, I felt pressure to finish grading while in my hospital room after having James and while he was in the NICU. I did that so no one could have any additional reason to comment on me negatively, including possible low student evaluation of teaching scores or negative comments due to grade delays. But that's not how stop-the-clock policies are supposed to work. People should be allowed and encouraged to actually take time away from their writing, from their responsibilities. Yet, if and when that happens, the pace of publications and research slows to a halt. As we've seen during the COVID-19 pandemic, completely stopping research requires that much more time to restart it, since even with already gathered data, articles take years to write and go through multiple rounds of peer review before actual publication. So stopping writing puts a freeze in the so-called publication pipeline resulting in fewer publications, which cannot be resolved by a simple promotion policy. Especially if these leaves are "gender neutral," scholars have shown how these policies actually benefit fathers because they use that time to publish more, thus increasing their tenure rates, and hurt mothers, who are unable to use that time to publish more, decreasing their tenure rates.[11] And even above and beyond the number of publications, using a stop-the-clock policy signals to other academics a lack of commitment to work.[12]

The lifeworlds of motherhood in US academia are informed by neoliberal logics of individualism. As a workplace, the academy operates as if motherhood, parenthood, and children are the result of individual choice; as such, academic workers are expected to deal with those consequences individually. Work-family conflicts are the responsibility of the faculty member, not the university.[13] As one faculty member put it in a department meeting: "We can't have different standards for different people." This faculty member's statement is a classic example of neoliberal understandings of individual choice and work. Yet equal treatment does not mean equal outcomes. Equality is not equity.

As Collins's work documents, these kinds of work-family struggles are not inevitable. Rather, they are "the result of cultural attitudes and policies embedded in workplaces and systems of welfare provisioning."[14] Even though scholars working in the university have produced reams of scholarship demonstrating the harms of these logics, the academic workplace continues to dismiss the needs of mother academics, particularly the needs of mothers of color. That's because the modern academy wasn't made for us. It was built on the assumption that faculty members would be white, married, heterosexual men whose spouses organized the care work for the family and the home, as well as the socializing labor that accompanies academic life. Academia was built on and continues to rely on the unpaid and unrecognized care work of its faculty members, graduate and undergraduate students, and staff.

Living in precarity is not an individual choice nor is it the fault of someone's own behavior. Rather, it is "a political outcome driven by power relations over and collective choices about how to distribute resources."[15] Charles Tilly describes how this "durable inequality"—or inequalities "that last from one social interaction to the next, with special attention to those that persist over whole careers, lifetimes, and organizational histories"—is based on a categorical differentiation of people.[16] These inequalities are created through exploitation and opportunity hoarding. They are cemented because people adapt to inequalities through daily practices and take policies, practices, and relationships from one setting and emulate them in a different setting.

The history of the global color line is a history of how these processes have played out.[17] From colonialism and the accompanying resource extraction by the colonizer from the colonized, to what Peter Evans calls "dependent development,"[18] and to what Cedric Robinson calls "racial capitalism,"[19] these and other processes maintain the durable inequalities between what's known as the Global North and the Global South.[20] Within the US, we also see these processes of exploitation, opportunity hoarding, emulation, and adaptation play out through schooling and housing, for example, where racism and racial discrimination have produced residential segregation,[21] and people of color—particularly Black families—lack generational wealth and the kinds of security and privilege it affords.

Racial capitalism, in other words, produces structural precarity by extracting value from racialized peoples and limiting their access to, and accumulation of, resources. It's tempting to think that these types of policies don't infiltrate or form the basis of universities and colleges. But they do. Precarity, especially racialized precarity, is bound up in their very structures.

I remember rushing down a hallway in a convention center, looking for a small room with a big white table in the center. I had been selected to participate in a focus group held by the Task Force on First Generation/Working Class Sociologists during the annual meeting of the American Sociological Association. As the professional society for sociologists, the ASA's annual meeting consists of research presentations, panels, workshops, seminars, a book fair, and the informal economies of academic life— coffees, dinners, and chats with colleagues across universities. This focus group included people of color who were first generation/working class sociologists.[22]

I arrived with plenty of time. Most of the chairs were still empty, so I selected one that was parallel to the door. I put my purse down to secure my spot and went to fill my water bottle. For the next hour, I felt kinship and seen with a group of Black and Brown sociologists I hadn't ever met but all of whom shared the same experiences and hurdles of academic life. Of putting purchases for everything from books to conference travel and attendance on credit cards. Of how the interest charged on these purchases got us deeper into debt. Of how this happened even to those of us with the privilege of having research funds, because research funds are often based on a reimbursement system. I knew this experience firsthand: I likely wouldn't get reimbursed for the registration fee, airfare, and lodging expenses that made it possible for me to be in that room for many months. And this reimbursement wouldn't cover all the things I actually paid for unless I used funds other than the UCR conference and travel grant I received.

Scholars often talk about precarity in the context of work, defined as "work that is uncertain, unstable, and insecure and in which employees bear the risks of work (as opposed to businesses or the government) and receive limited social benefits and statutory protections."[23] In academia, the term usually refers to the conditions for adjuncts, temporary faculty who work part-time and are paid by the credit hour or number of college courses they teach. The so-called academic precariat has grown from being 24% of the academic labor force in 1975 to 40% of the academic labor force in 2015.[24] They tend to be hired on a term basis, so what and whether they teach (and are paid) is constantly up in the air.

A report issued by the aforementioned ASA Task Force found that adjuncts often aren't given necessary teaching resources or space; that only about a quarter of them have health insurance; that everyday expenses associated with childcare, transportation, food, and housing can quickly spiral into financial crises; that adjuncts experience high stress and are at high risk for mental health issues; and that they often feel invisible in their profession.[25] O'Keefe and Courtois describe precarious workers (like adjuncts), especially women, as the "non-citizens" of the university because they occupy a type of four-pronged nonstatus in terms of staff recognition or support, decision-making, social standing, and work recognition.[26]

The academic precariat is a racialized underclass. In 2013, for example, the TIAA Institute found that almost 60% of all underrepresented minority faculty were in part-time positions and that part-time positions make up just over half of all faculty jobs.[27] So although the number of faculty of color (particularly Black, Latinx, and Indigenous faculty) entering the profession is increasing, this is occurring as part-time work. Precarity, and its effects, are also gendered, negatively affecting women's careers more than men's.[28]

The task force that had brought us together that day had expertise on the particular forms of precarity affecting adjunct and non-tenure-track faculty, but many of us did not fall into that category (though some may have). We were graduate students, tenure-track, and even tenured faculty. Yet, we continued to live paycheck to paycheck, even going into debt to be able to pursue our intellectual careers. Academic inequities persist, in part, because not everyone enters the academy with the same resources or hurdles—those who are white, privileged, and have access to generational wealth do not experience work and life in the same way as those who are part of the 43.2 million[29] people (who tend to be people of color and white women[30]) saddled with overwhelming student debt. This has implications even for those who secure the coveted tenure-track position. But not all tenure-track positions are created equal.

Research universities (R1s, as they are popularly known) evaluate their tenure-track faculty on the basis of research, teaching and service—but mostly research. Faculty in these institutions tend to be the highest paid. After that, in order of academic prestige (but not necessarily pay because of unionized contracts), you have the selective liberal arts colleges, R2s (directional colleges, for example), liberal arts colleges that aren't as selective, community colleges, and many others. There are pay differences among faculty who work at these varied institutions, but also between faculty at the same institution. The status hierarchy places R1 faculty at the top and community college faculty at the bottom.

Differences abound even within the often coveted R1 universities. In their 2021 book *Broke: The Racial Consequences of Underfunding Public Universities,* Laura Hamilton and Kelly Nielsen document how even the prestigious, research-based University of California system is a racialized hierarchy, one that places Berkeley at the top, which enrolls "the lowest percentage of Latinx and Black students."[31] UCLA is a close second, and both Berkeley and UCLA "have the lowest percentage of Pell

Grant recipients in the system."[32] This racialized hierarchy also places the Riverside and Merced campuses on the bottom. These two campuses primarily serve the needs of Black and Brown students and lack even basic facilities and infrastructure common in the whiter and richer UCs. These funding decisions are driven by austerity logics and practices that entrench racial inequalities between UC campuses.[33]

On paper, I make a good living. My annual salary from my one job is over four times what my grandma made working three jobs when I was growing up. Yet, I still live paycheck to paycheck, and I don't have any savings. My grandma, daughter, son and I live in Riverside, across the street from the Canyon Crest Towne Center. It's a place where we can walk to get groceries. It has my and my daughter's dentist offices, a donut store where my grandma can get her lottery ticket, a Starbucks, a local bookstore owned by a friend, and a Hallmark store where my daughter loves to go in and look at all the stuffed animals. Rent for our two-bedroom townhouse eats up a third of my monthly paycheck. Factor in bills, paying my grandma a few hundred dollars a month because she cooks, cleans, and helps care for my kids, and sending money to family in the Philippines,[34] and I run out of money by mid-month. My kids' father sends money each month to help take care of them. Without that money, we couldn't get by. But his contributions just cover daycare. And here I am, on the cusp of tenure at what is supposed to be a R1 university. Yet I can't make ends meet through my paycheck alone.

Frederick Wherry, Kristin Seefeldt, and Anthony Alvarez use the term "financial citizenship" to describe how "full members of a financialized society, [are able to] assert their freedom *from* and their rights *to:* their freedom *from* exploitation, and their right *to* recognition, social belonging and the co-creation of institutions of commerce."[35] These rights include "being protected from deception and coercion," "being treated as if one's decisions are valid," "being able to use credit and debt in order to participate in family and community rituals; being able to treat requests from loved ones as valid (relational rights)," and "the freedom to use expertise from both local, unofficial practices and official, nonlocal practices . . . to make new hybrid products and services."[36] Their focus is on the racialized history of markets and on how the structure of debt, credit, and finance widen inequalities, which precludes many from full financial citizenship.

Academic life is similarly structured. Scholars often treat publications as the quasi-currency of intellectual life that opens the doors for jobs, fellowships, grants, and awards, but academic economies take multiple forms—including actual dollars. These distinctions start even before the first paycheck, with moving expenses. Will moving costs be covered, and, if so, will they be paid directly through the university, or are they reimbursed? Some faculty can get funding for down payments for their homes, while others receive no such thing. Some universities offer low-interest loans to faculty as a perk of the job, while others do not. These differences in compensation packets reflect not only differences in university resources, but also because academic job offers at nonunionized campuses are based on individual negotiations, which privilege white men and disadvantage everyone else.

Academic economies also revolve around research expenses—whether used to buy books or hire student assistants—and attendance at conferences. In nonpandemic times, attending an academic conference usually costs upwards of $1,000, including association membership, meeting registration, airfare, a hotel stay, and food and drinks during the conference. And that estimate holds for conferences held even in areas with low costs of living. The expenses dramatically increase when they are held in cities with high costs of living, where conferences tend to be held because those same cities attract the most conference attendees. The shift to virtual meetings has reduced these costs somewhat, but participants often still have to pay hundreds of dollars in membership and registration fees to participate and access the full program. Faculty usually pay all costs upfront. Although many, but not all, faculty, can use research funds to help cover the costs, we cannot get reimbursed until after the conference is over. Since I don't have an extra $1,000 to attend a conference, that means I put all the costs on my credit card, which then racks up interest that university funds don't cover. Not that the allotted $750 I regularly receive for conference and travel comes anywhere near covering the total cost. For the rest, I end up getting reimbursement from my start-up funds or, more likely, paying out of pocket. Between attending multiple conferences and hiring undergraduate students as research assistants, I depleted my start-up funds within my first three years.

But I can't just not go. Nor would I want to stay behind, because I actually enjoy conferences and the intimate economies[37] of academia—those coffees and dinners that revolve around them. It's how I've found my support network. It also facilitates, in both direct and subtle ways, co-authorships, jobs, letters of recommendation, and the like. I am then forced to choose between racking up debt or not developing and maintaining professional relationships. And yet, I am expected to maintain exactly these kinds of professional relationships, which can be attained only by spending money I do not have, to get tenure. They also help make me feel as though I belong in the profession.

It is precisely through these negotiated interactional orders, their multiple local and extra local meanings—what scholars call their "inhabited institutionalism"[38] —that limit academic citizenship to those who can afford it. Living in precarity means having to choose between existing on the edges, remaining excluded from academic life and full participation, which comes at great financial cost. Insiders face no such choice.

OVERLAPPING SHIFTS AND COVID-19

A good day during the first sixteen months of the COVID-19 pandemic means having a babysitter for Olivia, even if that means money is extra tight. I wake up between 5 and 5:30 a.m., grab the exercise clothes I laid out the night before, and try to open the door to the room we share without waking her up. She's only just started sleeping in her own bed, a loft bed with a slide located at the foot of my own bed. Since I'm describing a good day, let's assume she doesn't wake up. I carefully move down the stairs to the living room in the dark before stumbling into the kitchen to grab a yogurt, still rubbing my eyes. I sit down for anywhere from fifteen minutes to half an hour, all the while scrolling on my phone. I brush my teeth downstairs and change into my workout gear.

I put on my shoes and socks, take my daily dose of Zoloft, put on my headphones, and head out the door for my run. When I get back, if I'm lucky, everyone is still asleep, and I can shower and eat breakfast in peace.

Or maybe Olivia's up, having already used her iPad to Skype me to come home. Either way, the kids are officially up somewhere between 7:30 and 8 a.m. I go upstairs to bring them back down, change James's diaper, get him milk, fix breakfast for Olivia, and convince them both to brush their teeth. Both kids sleep in the clothes they'll wear the next day to alleviate the burden and stress of changing clothes in the morning. I tell Olivia to set up her table for virtual school, which starts at 8:30 a.m. We stay downstairs together for a bit while my grandma goes for her morning walk. During this time, I try to write emails, but James generally doesn't let me, pushing my laptop or phone down, crossing his arms to say no, and tugging me to play with him. So I don't really get anything done.

Around 9:45 a.m., Olivia is on break from school, and my grandma generally gets back from her walk. I can finally go upstairs to get ready for my first meeting of the day, which I try to never schedule before 10 a.m. Whatever I'm doing at 10:15, I have to stop to call Olivia to come back to school. She spends the rest of the day of her virtual school at a desk under her loft bed, sitting next to me and my makeshift office, a space in the small corner between the closet and her bed. I can never quite focus on whatever I'm trying to do—hold a meeting, prep for teaching, or write—because I have to constantly remind Olivia to pay attention to school and turn down the volume on her iPad. On less good days, I have to take her iPad away from her. Her school lasts until 11:30 a.m., when she usually goes downstairs for lunch that Grandma made.

On good days, I then have an hour to myself for uninterrupted work.

This ends around 12:30 p.m., when James usually comes up to give me a kiss and tell me to come downstairs so his ate[1] isn't alone. I pick him up and bring him to the room he shares with Grandma. While they settle in for their nap, I go downstairs to eat lunch and have Olivia do twenty to thirty minutes of homework. Then—this is a good day—the sitter comes.

The three hours from 1 to 4 p.m., when someone else is taking care of my children, are precious. But since it's also the only extended uninterrupted time I get, I have to squeeze everything into this small window, including reading, writing, grading, prepping for classes, answering emails, meeting with my research team, meeting with my writing group, commenting on graduate students' papers, writing letters of recommendation, reviewing articles, coordinating service (for example, being on a committee), and any number of other things on the never-ending list of things I'm behind on, that I need to do, and could barely get started during the hour between Olivia finishing her school and James coming upstairs to get me. If there's anything I need to do in the outside world without my kids, this three-hour window is the only time it can happen. And there are lots of things I'd prefer to do without them, since even going to the post office—let alone the grocery store—takes twice as long and requires at least twice as much energy if they're with me. After the sitter leaves, Olivia does another half hour of homework. Then dinner, more homework with Olivia, then play and TV with the kids until it's time to get ready for bed.

One of my favorite routines is at night, in part because its success doesn't depend on access to a babysitter nor does it involve added pressure. It's a routine that marks the end of a day and one that brings me joy. I go into the bathroom to put face wash on, and James brings a stool to stand next to me. Together, we floss our teeth. Or, more accurately, I floss and he tries. After one or two teeth, he generally abandons the floss and says "help momma"— meaning please throw the floss in the trashcan, I'm done with it and what can I do to help you. I tell him that we have to wash our faces, so I wash mine and he washes his. Afterward, I put on moisturizer, and he does the same. Once that's finished, he gives me my toothpaste to put on my toothbrush. As I brush my teeth, he smiles at me, does a little dance or tries to find something else he can do to his face before we both leave the bathroom The kids play for a bit. James goes to sleep in the room he shares with grandma, and I follow him in to say and kiss him goodnight. Olivia comes to the room that we share. When her closely negotiated iPad time expires, I climb into her loft bed to chat about our day. We stare out the window, watching the view, listening for the skateboarder who passes by our window around that time, and sharing our favorite and least favorite moments of the day. Our first answer to our favorite movement of today is always, for both of us, "right now"—by which we mean talking with one another. After chatting, I climb back down to my bed. Because she can't sleep without me in the same room, I lay in my bed, usually falling asleep in exhaustion around the same time she does. If I'm able to stay up until after Olivia falls asleep, I go downstairs, often staying awake until past midnight to binge TV shows I cannot watch at any other time. The next morning, around 5 or 5:30 a.m., it all starts again.

This is a good day. A day that is not great, but not bad, might also have doctors' appointments, whether for me, my grandma, or the kids, meetings before 1 or after 4, or calls with family, whether in the US or the Philippines, requesting money or passing along some other drama. It might also involve my daughter literally hanging upside down from her loft bed during virtual school but getting down as soon as I ask. A bad day might include screams, yelling, or fits thrown by one or both kids, which can last all day, through each session of homework, whenever I ask them to do something, or all night. Bad days are days, weeks, or months at a time when I can't get a sitter. On the worst days, the phone calls share news of a family member's illness or death. Lately, it feels like the bad days outnumber the good. When there are too many bad days in a row, I break down. Olivia's screams and yelling, telling me she doesn't want me in the family, trigger me in a deep way. When I can't take the screaming or yelling any more, I have to walk away or take my frustration and anger upstairs. The most random and smallest things seem to upset her the most, but I have to remember that she, too, is exhausted, stretched thin, and can't take being cooped up anymore. In this, she's like children across the world.[2]

The COVID-19 pandemic has collapsed any sense of boundary between work and home life.[3] Instead, it has demanded that mothers and other types of caregivers work *overlapping shifts*. Each and every responsibility demands attention at the same time.[4] The roles overlap, bleeding together and leaving caregivers—myself included—unable to really do any job well. I feel like I'm failing at everything, whether it's the research, teaching, or service demanded by my paid employment, or the elder care and childcare needed at home.

This sense of failing at everything, of watching my career sail by and my kids' mental and emotional well-being collapse, all while feeling like I can't do anything about any of it, leaves me feeling utterly lost and alone. But, of course, I am not alone, not even close to it. Working mothers across the academy share similar struggles and have been the ones most affected by COVID-19.[5] And the academy is only a small slice. Across industries, women are disappearing from the workplace, as women lost an estimated 64 million jobs globally in 2020, 5% of all jobs held by women,[6] and a survey of 5,000 women across the globe found that "seventy-seven percent of women report that their workload has increased and fifty-one percent feel less optimistic about their career prospects today than before the pandemic. LGBTQ+ women and women of color are even more likely to report lower levels of mental wellbeing and work-life balance."[7]

And, yet, despite all of this, universities have expected their faculty to mostly continue functioning as if everything is normal. But it is not. And the present is unsustainable.

I drafted above paragraphs in the summer of 2020 and finished revisions in early 2022. Our routines have shifted remarkably since then, even as uncertainty and worry continue to pervade our lives. As of January 2022, it's been three months since both kids are back at school. But it doesn't feel like it, especially when one or both kids get sick, which involves testing them for COVID-19 (negative so far) and staying home for days at a time until they are symptom-free. Or when James's daycare shuts down for a week due to a widespread COVID outbreak. I feel like I'm still drowning. Overlapping shifts are still the norm. I can't catch up or return to any semblance of "normal" life, pre-COVID. It still often takes me anywhere from two days to two weeks or more to answer even the most basic email.

The damage has been cumulative. My life and the lives of so many others have been shattered into a million tiny pieces that cannot be glued back into their rightful places. Pieces are still missing; the cracks cannot be covered up. I am not alone.

The COVID-19 pandemic alongside the renewed attention and mass mobilization against anti-Black racism and increasing support for the Black Lives Matter movement have revealed—to some, for the first time—that global relations are built on foundations of systemic racism[8] and other existing inequalities.[9] These inequities persist and deepen because, as sociologist Whitney N. Laster Pirtle[10] argues, racial capitalism is a major cause of health disparities. But the pandemic has not just revealed these inequities; it has deepened and entrenched them.

The combined crises of 2020 and 2021 have made the costs associated with prolonged crisis management, precarity, and high-stress living situations visible to many people who have never been confronted with them before. But I worry that once these people, particularly white, middle-class people, regain a sense of normality— once their kids are back in school and they've established a routine of either remote or in-person work—that their concern for the stress, precarity, and difficult living situations for others will fade in the background. And when and if that happens, it's because their concern wasn't really for society writ large, or how governments and people have collectively responded to the pandemic. It was about themselves.

Indeed, this is what I see happening. The social media feeds of many of my white, middle-class friends have reverted back to posting about their baking experiments and family trips to the forest or beach. I noticed that they began posting back-to-school photos in January or February 2021, even as my daughter—and many of her classmates—remained in virtual school for the entire 2020–2021 school year. We enrolled her in virtual school because of safety concerns for Olivia, my grandmother, and others who are vulnerable in our community, despite in-person school being an option.

In many ways, we were privileged to be able to choose to remain virtual, though that choice wasn't really a choice because choosing face-to-face instruction would have involved sending Olivia into the unknown before vaccines were available. It would have involved the very real possibility of her bringing home a virus that would kill my grandmother. And although I "can" work at home in that I am not an essential worker and am able to theoretically accomplish much of my work online, the cumulative weight of prolonged virtual school has wrought a powerful cost.

On the other hand, many who "chose" face-to-face instruction because they are essential workers aren't given a choice either. They have to go into work and send their children into the school system despite any fears or uneasiness. Some people don't have a choice of whether to go back to face-to-face or remain virtual because government officials pressure schools to return to in-person instruction. The same government officials who refuse to back or issue a mask and vaccine mandate, leaving the communities they are supposed to serve vulnerable. Almost at the two-year mark of the nationwide (and global) shutdown, people are pressured to go into work, regardless of whether they've been exposed to someone infected with COVID or even if they've tested positive themselves.

The pandemic has exacerbated and amplified every inequity in our society, particularly those related to race and gender. Whitney N. Laster Pirtle and Tashelle Wright describe structural gendered racism as "the totality of interconnectedness between structural racism and structural sexism in shaping race and gender inequities" and argue that structural gendered racism is a root cause of inequities for Black women and women of color.[11] So it's no surprise that the white families I see on my social media timelines seem to be handling things so much better than me. It's because they *are* in a structurally better position than me and many of my friends. COVID-19 has disproportionately impacted the communities I'm a part of, not theirs. These circumstances are not a coincidence.

Every other week I want to cry. My eyes are a reservoir, filled just below the rim. The moment something happens, it overflows. I get frustrated and need time alone. All I ask is for time by myself, to not have my kids crawling on me, touching me, or calling on me to play or help them with something. When it overflows, I can no longer hide from my feelings; my anger, frustration, and exhaustion come out. For the next day or two, I'll be fine because the water is once again below the rim. But I'm not really fine. But what choice do I have? This is my life for the foreseeable future, for the health and safety of my family.

The ongoing, constantly high stress is not healthy. Stress manifests physically.[12] Even more so, it seems, as you get older. One day in summer 2020, I woke up and it hurt to walk. This new physical pain appeared a few days after the mental and emotional pain of a string of particularly contentious faculty meetings, faculty emails, and department-wide listserv exchanges, where some faculty members, who were eager to write a supportive statement of Black Lives Matter mobilizations, were also against any kind of institutional or structural change that would benefit current and potential Black students in the department. Weeks after George Floyd was murdered, some of these same faculty also attempted to push through a department code of conduct that our graduate students were required to sign, without any faculty discussion. The code of conduct, on the surface, read as "reasonable" in terms of being respectful of others and against climates that are intimidating or harassing, but in practice these same words have historically been mobilized as a weapon against those who bring up concerns about racism and sexism. So, too, did some members of the department draft a plan to address graduate students concerns about racism and sexism in the department, which initially included similar language that students would pledge not to talk "badly" about faculty members to one another. Students talking "badly" about some faculty was what concerned them. Not that some faculty members created hostile climates for students (and other faculty). That's because the people placed in charge of drafting the plan were those, in my opinion, often creating such a climate.

After I woke up that morning, every step was painful. I started using a cane. The days went by but still, nothing but pain whenever I walked. On Facebook, two women of color friends recommended acupuncture. I tried it. The pain diminished almost immediately; after a few sessions, the pain receded entirely. At least for a few days. For the rest of the summer, my biweekly appointments to the acupuncturist were one of the few times I left the house by myself.

The situation is bad for everyone, but the particular demands of academic employment have exacerbated my pandemic-related physical, mental, and emotional stress. That's because the academic workplace hires, rewards, and promotes people on the basis of individual merit, rather than considering the costs of collective, gendered racism and harm people of color face on a daily basis in their workplace, much less during a global, deadly pandemic. Neither does it value the labor it takes to address gendered racial injustice on campus and in mass mobilizations.

Alt-right politicians decry academia as a liberal hotbed. But in my experience, and many others', it's conservative and resistant to change. Even as many colleagues (at my university or another) are kind, compassionate, and understanding during this time of a global pandemic that has killed close to a million Americans at the time of this writing, and while vigilantes and police murder Black people, others are not so compassionate.[13] They demand the same kinds of (quick) labor that they expected before the pandemic; some of them seem to expect even more rapid responses than before. They dismiss what's going on in the world and the impact of these events on people's lives, demanding the same expectations and labor of undergraduate students in their courses, graduate students in their research progress and teaching commitments, and even colleagues' research, teaching, and service responsibilities. Some administrators have discussed making the use of student evaluations (which we know are biased) optional during the pandemic, while others still want to reward those teachers who go "above and beyond"—as if teaching and mentoring during a global pandemic is not already going "above and beyond." All of this just compounds the increasing stress I feel each day.[14]

And yet, these faculty members and administrators are not an anomaly. Their actions and words aren't individual "quirks." Rather they are made possible by the structural and cultural assumptions of academic life, which are centered on individual merit, including flexible and independent schedules (which, in practice, means work emails are often sent without regard to time and outside nine-to-five business hours). Assumptions that were built around, and for, white, married, heterosexual cis men.

Even early in the pandemic, scholars already knew that COVID-19 would disproportionately impact women faculty, especially those who are mothers, of color, and/or those with younger children.[15] Scholars concerned about equity in academia provided advice to mentors, university administrators, scientific societies, publishers, institution leaders, funding agencies, and faculty on how to mitigate these effects of the pandemic on underrepresented scholars' careers. And they continue to do so. These strategies are varied, including everything from having faculty write statements on the impact of COVID on their research, teaching, and service; to having mentors advocate for mentees; to encouraging scientific societies and publishers to extend their deadlines; to encouraging administrators to pause tenure clocks; to providing financial assistance for caregivers and clearinghouses to help campus community members find caregivers.[16] Many institutions have acted on at least some of this advice, in some cases providing tenure-track faculty with additional research funds to help mitigate the pandemic's effects.

This advice is well-meaning. On paper, it seems to provide paths forward. In practice, however, the strategies provide language of inclusion without actually committing to how true equity requires a fundamental rethinking of the academy. All the advice and resources or accommodations provided are about propping up a merit-based system, which assumes that individual evaluation is, in fact, the best way to make decisions about hiring and promotion, even during a global pandemic and even when we know that the tools we use (for example, student evaluations of teaching, which journals papers are published in, the quantity of scholarship) and the very understanding of what constitutes "merit" and "excellence" are based on foundations of gendered racism. Yet it doesn't have to be that way. Instead, academy can start from a position of care, or what Zakiya Luna and Whitney N. Laster Pirtle call a "loving sociology," which would stem from asking "what do our employees need to survive and thrive?" It would involve approaching members of campus communities as valued.

Not asking them in the midst of a deadly pandemic to prove their need for accommodations. At their worst, accommodations backfire, exacerbating inequities as delayed tenure or research has a cumulative effect and will continue to impact a person's file for years to come.

My university, for example, offers faculty members an opportunity to draft a statement for their tenure packet explaining COVID's effects on their output. I started mine by factually describing my circumstances, since the context of how COVID impacted my life is necessary to understand the virus's effects on my job. After this, I pivoted to detailing COVID's direct impact on my research, teaching, and service. This material made up the bulk of my one-page statement. Soon after I submitted my statement, a staff member reached out to tell me that my statement was "too personal." I was advised that I shouldn't include details about my home life. Fortunately, my new department chair encouraged me to leave the statement as is, as this would be the only chance to make my case.

Nor is it clear to me what this statement is for in practice. This same staff person who told me to revise the statement also told me that it would not be circulated to external readers. A faculty member's tenure file consists of a packet of statements, publications, and similar evidence of a scholar's research, teaching, and service accomplishments. The department chair sends the packet to tenured, external faculty who are asked to review and assess the materials, ultimately making a recommendation as to whether the faculty member should receive tenure. The point of a COVID impact statement is to explain how the pandemic might have affected a scholar's output, but the university apparently did not plan to include the statement with the file. I followed up, asking high-level administrators about this apparent gap between the purpose of the COVID impact statement and how it was currently being used. One person responded, copying another, asking the same question. That was the last I heard about the issue.

I shared my statement on Twitter's public stage, asking whether it was too personal. Most people thought not, but at least one recommended I tally all the hours lost because of the coronavirus. This person explained that COVID's effects would be more legible to my university's Committee on Academic Personnel if they were quantifiable. Faculty members on this committee, which reviews merits and promotions across the university, are required to hold the rank of full professor. As such, they also tend to be white men, which means they are less likely to be personally impacted by the pandemic. That's because they are older so less likely to have young children or if they do, are more financially stable and able to hire childcare if they need it. They are also less likely to be living in intergenerational housing situations or with family in service jobs or essential work positions that increase their exposure to the virus and have better access to generational wealth that would cushion their circumstances if their partner lost their job. This list can go on.

Indeed, I've seen and read about how these kinds of professors talk about how they have more time to write during the pandemic and have increased their productivity. One of the surprising (but not really) findings of the pandemic is that journal submissions have increased.[17] Despite conversations to change this model, few journals are tracking the race/ethnicity, gender, and other characteristics of authors and reviewers. An exception is Flaminio Squazzoni and colleagues[18] who were able to collect data on the gender of authors for over two thousand Elsevier journals, and their work finds that women have submitted proportionately fewer manuscripts than men. To take this further and based on what we know, it's reasonable to suggest that it is white men who are increasing productivity, while women of color, mothers of color, white mothers, and others from marginalized communities who have increased caregiving and other sorts of responsibilities during the pandemic have not, and these people are the ones who are and will continue to be harmed for years to come.

I'd seen this suggestion to document COVID's impacts via quantifiable hours in research reports and op-eds; it's not uncommon advice. Yet, it also makes me want to scream. I'm too exhausted. How much time would it take to make those calculations? How much labor should I put into explaining why I'm so far behind? Putting efforts into making these calculations loses the precious few hours that I—and others in similar positions—have to do our actual work: the research, teaching, and service required of us, all in a context where 1 in 100 Americans over sixty-five have died from COVID.[19]

I get frustrated even with well-meaning advice that comes from presumably a good place. It conveys that I wouldn't have this problem if only I did _____.[20] Or that I can secure my place at the university if I only did more labor (such as providing more documentation).[21] Either situation implies that *I* am the problem, that it's on me to fix the situation. If only, if only, if only...

I've done all that I can and more. It's not about what more I can do. And even if I—as an individual—have a "strong enough" tenure file without any accommodations, what about all of the others, all the caregivers and outsiders, who need for the situation, for systems, to change in order to achieve that elusive tenured status? We need other people to give a damn and enact change. But that would require change from the very people who resist change the most, many of whom refuse to even recognize the problem. That's because it's never been plausible to expect people with caregiving responsibilities and who deal with gendered racism in the workplace to match the "scholarly productivity" of people who either have fewer responsibilities or have material resources to relieve them of their duties. To expect the same outcomes despite different obstacles is the opposite of equity.

And yet, we know that social change in any context doesn't come without struggle and without a fight, whether the freeing of enslaved Black Americans, voting rights, citizenship rights, marriage rights, bodily autonomy, and decolonization, all of which continue to be under attack to this day, among so many other struggles. Frederick Douglass, a Black abolitionist and author who was originally born into enslavement, stated in an 1857 speech that "power concedes nothing without a demand. It never did and it never will. Find out just what any people will quietly submit to and you have found out the exact measure of injustice and wrong which will be imposed upon them, and these will continue till they are resisted with either words or blows, or with both."[22] Douglass gave this speech five years before the Emancipation Proclamation, the executive order issued by President Abraham Lincoln that changed the legal status of enslaved Black peoples to free Black peoples. 165 years after Douglass's speech, his words continue to ring true, as mass mobilizations such as #BlackLivesMatter show. And although the rights of faculty of color, and in particular mothers of color, in the academy are far from the issue of Black enslavement, systemic gendered racism means that equity and full, unconditional citizenship in any sphere is a process of constant struggle.

Therefore, unless and until university administrators come to understand that the status quo is untenable, I am skeptical that any amount of extra documentation will allow faculty mothers and others severely impacted by the pandemic to pass through the tenure and promotion process as if the past two years did not happen. Nor does it seem likely that those scholars who paused their research and publication pipelines to participate in movements against anti-Black racism will have much of a chance on the job market against those scholars who continued to publish as if nothing had happened. These inequities will continue and deepen, and it's important to remember that should not be surprising, as the academy is operating exactly as it was intended: to privilege the few for whom it was built.

We're now about to begin the third year of the COVID-19 pandemic. I'm still here, inside, exhausted, groping around in the dark for time and quiet away from two young kids who crave my undivided attention—including even my body, wanting to jump on or over me, for me to carry them—throughout the day. While I long to give that to them, I'm unable. Not only because of the overlapping shifts I deal with, but also because I am beyond burned out. I am depleted. The only things that have kept me sane (literally: I suffer from chronic severe depression) are writing these essays and sharing my struggles via texts and talks with friends.

I'm also filled with anger. The words of Black feminist poet Audre Lorde have taught me to embrace my anger, to recognize its righteousness and its power. She writes, "My anger is a response to racist attitudes and to the actions and presumptions that arise out of those attitudes . . . We operate in the teeth of a system for which racism and sexism are primary, established and necessary props of profit...[and] Anger is an appropriate reaction to racist attitudes, as is fury when the actions arising from those attitudes do not change."[23] The process of writing this book has been fueled by the anger—the fury—that grows from the entrenched racism and sexism I encounter every day in the academy. I can no longer stay silent.

Whatever privileges I had prior to the pandemic have been stripped from me. I lie bare in my wounds, exhaustion, and hurt. And still, I am confronted every day with excuses, lack of change, inertia.

We are now living in a potentially transformative moment of history, one that includes both the largest civil rights protests in US history and a global pandemic the likes of which hasn't been seen since the 1918 influenza pandemic infected an estimated 500 million people (about one-third of the estimated global population).[24] At the first debate of the 2020 presidential election, a sitting US president refused to denounce white supremacy and called for a white supremist group to "stay back and stand by," and in January 2021, some of his supporters stormed the US Capitol in an attempted coup to try to keep him in office.[25] They failed. This time. President Joe Biden and Vice President Kamala Harris, the latter of whom is the first Black woman and first Asian American woman to hold the office, are now the elected leaders of this country. If there was ever a time for structural and radical change to take hold, it is now. But this kind of change relies on people in power recognizing that the current crisis is only part of a much longer, systemic crisis that has been afflicting those of us on the outside—outside mainstream US white society, academia, or whatever job or profession we are in but in which we don't belong. Not merely recognizing: doing something about it.

One year into the new administration, I am not optimistic.

Yet, while of course it's better to have these kinds of policies come from the top, most transformative changes—the kind of changes we desperately need to combat structural gendered racism—never come from those who already hold power. They come from the people who demand change. Although I'm privileged to have some social support (and without which, I'm not sure whether I literally could have survived this pandemic), I've simultaneously long felt alone during this pandemic. Yet, in reality, there are so many people who similarly feel devastatingly alone and abandoned. What will happen when we see our pain as collective and together demand change?

I've grown increasingly disillusioned about the academy. Bitter and resentful with the lack of accountability for the gendered racism and sexism tenured faculty perpetuate or enable. I never thought that I would be here, pushed to the brink. Where I think about leaving academia because of entrenched racism, sexism, and toxicity. Academia is a place where even so-called white allies shrug their shoulders and defend an institution's racist and sexist policies. At best, they send emails after meetings in support of what I've (or others have) said. Meanwhile, when presented with opportunities to effect change, or at least show their support in public, they do nothing.

I feel pushed out of sociology precisely because I love my job. All aspects of it—the research and the writing, teaching and mentoring, and service toward the communities I care about. But I cannot stay in a place that harms me, physically, emotionally, and intellectually. A place whose harms are manifesting in the kinds of physical pain that keeps me from being able to walk. I feel pushed out, forced to choose between my well-being and employment in a disciplinary department.

I recently moved my full-time equivalent (FTE) line from the Department of Sociology to the Department of Gender and Sexualities Studies. The decision and ability to transfer were a long time coming, not something decided on a whim. I was not worried about being denied tenure. It was that I increasingly did not *want* tenure in that department.

With that decision came a sigh of relief, but also anxiety and a fear of losing status and my professional identity. At my core, I think of myself as a sociologist. That's how I've been trained, how I think and how I write. But as many scholars have noted, people (often cis white men who are staunch disciplinary traditionalists) too frequently push marginalized scholars out of disciplinary departments.[1] These same people also look down on those of us who hold appointments in interdisciplinary departments.[2] That's because scholars in these settings—we—are seen as failing to secure, or not being good enough for, a disciplinary job. I've had close friends who expressed shock and sorrow at my leaving the sociology department but go on to reassure me that people will still see me as a sociologist. I have also heard people say about those who have left a sociology department that those people (who tend to be scholars of color and/or queer scholars) were "not really" sociologists or their work was "not really" sociology to begin with, so the interdisciplinary department that they moved to was a better fit. I know and anticipate the stigma attached to leaving a disciplinary department. I have to battle the feeling that I'm a failure for not being able to "tough" it out.

But what would a sociology department, and the academy more generally, look like if it didn't push people out? If sociology as a profession, and disciplinary departments more generally, sought to *keep and retain* people, rather than perpetuating a constant cycle of hiring marginalized faculty, subjecting them to racism and sexism, gaslighting them when they raise concerns, and driving them out, only to ask the administration for more hires and repeat the cycle again and again?

Alternatively, what would the academy look like if it valued interdisciplinary departments? After all, many university and college administrators tout the mantra of valuing interdisciplinary thinking. And interdisciplinary departments like Ethnic Studies, African American/Black Studies, Asian American Studies, Latinx Studies, Native American Indian/Indigenous Studies, and Women and Gender Studies are where many—perhaps even most—faculty from marginalized communities are employed and were created as a direct result of student demands to center the histories and scholarship of communities of color. 3 What if universities and colleges poured as many resources into these departments—that is, fund as many faculty and staff positions; match research funds, summer salaries, and course buyouts; and commit the same amount of graduate student funding and positions—as they do for disciplinary priorities?

What if the academy took up Adia Harvey Wingfield's call for organizations to be "driven by a race-conscious approach that recognizes the challenges facing workers of color and assumes responsibility for resolving them"?[4]

I feel a bit disingenuous in writing something hopeful, as for the past few years I've been filled with frustration and pain. But I nevertheless try to latch onto Sara Ahmed's words, that "hope is not at the expense of struggle but animates a struggle...[it] carries us through when the terrain is difficult, when the path we follow makes it hard to proceed. Hope is behind us when we have to work for something to be possible."[5] This is because hope is not a thought or fleeting feeling, but "a philosophy of living," according to organizer, educator, and curator Mariame Kaba. She reminds us that "hope is a discipline and that we have to practice it every single day."[6] Hope is tied to action; it cannot exist without it. Rebecca Solnit describes hope without action as optimism—belief that things will be okay, whether or not we do anything about them. Instead, to hope is to believe "that what we do matters even though how and when it may matter, who and what it may impact, are not things we can know beforehand."[7]

It is nearly impossible for most of us to imagine an academy without hierarchy, racism, sexism, or exclusion of any kind. And yet, we still have to try. We must ask ourselves: What, then, is possible for the academy? What are its potentials? How can we hope for a just academy? What would *academic justice* look like in practice?

I am not the first to ask these questions. Many scholars, particularly feminists of color, have struggled, fought for, and imagined what academic justice could look like in practice.[8]

I use the term *academic justice* to denote a system where all members of the academy—from undergraduates and graduate students to postdocs, lecturers, and tenure-stream faculty—are able to fully partake in an academic life free from microaggressions, discrimination, and racist and sexist abuse; one filled with support and acknowledgment of the value and worth of our ideas, research, and backgrounds; and one that provides living wages, healthcare, and resources for our labor. Academic justice means that everyone is granted rights and seen as worthy; no one's citizenship is conditional.[9] As Black activist Fannie Lou Hamer said, "Nobody's free until everyone's free."[10]

Academic justice requires centering academic life around the principles of Black Feminist Sociology (BFS). This goes for sociologists and nonsociologists alike. Zakiya Luna and Whitney N. Laster Pirtle state that BFS is "creative, undefined, transformative, humanizing, and loving."[11] Abiding by these principles would mean trusting Black women, attending to joy, remaining mindful of ethics, and remembering "that knowledge is a collective process"[12] that requires uplifting one another. BFS enacts

Black author Toni Morrison's call to action, that "the function of freedom is to free somebody else."[13]

A loving Black feminist sociology has a long tradition, as Luna and Pirtle note. The late Black feminist scholar bell hooks, for example, describes love "as the will to nurture our own and another's spiritual growth,"[14] where "a commitment to a spiritual life . . . requires conscious practice, a willingness to unite the way we think with the way we act."[15] She expands that "without justice there can be no love"[16] since "a love ethic presupposes that everyone has the right to be free, to live fully and well."[17]

What would it mean to create an academy—or any workplace—built on love? Not a love that results in unevenly distributed resources, withheld from those dissimilar from those already in power. Rather, a love centered on distributing resources and recognition equitably, and that fosters the value and worth of each person, regardless of their status and rank? One where we also live our intellectual life with integrity, which bell hooks describes as "present when our behavior is congruent with our professed values, when ideals and practice match."[18]

I ponder hooks's words whenever I am confronted by everyday decisions, big and small alike, that involve interactions with others. Whether it's something in the classroom, like students asking for extensions on top of the extensions I've already given; in my research, making sure I'm not only referring to work by "famous" scholars or published in elite sociology journals; or in my service work in committees, rereading papers or books that people submit to award committees to identify strengths when they're not obvious on first read. Integrity in one does not negate the need for integrity in the other. And these thoughts about integrity, and whether I have any, linger inside me and push me to action, even and especially when my own initial reactions prompt me toward self-protection and being on the defense. Because I don't always live up to these ideals. Even though I try. And when we fail—because we will, I will—what matters is how we respond. Instead of doubling down in defense, we must find empathy, understanding, and a commitment to change our actions and be better.

For academic work to be led by love, integrity, and justice means not allowing hollow words and commitments to stand in place of actual change. It would mean putting into practice our understanding of the differences between equity and equality. Equality gives everyone access to equal resources without addressing the different ways those resources are felt. Equity not only acknowledges the uneven playing field but addresses it by providing different resources or abolishing obstacles. Academic justice would mean implementing policies like providing all faculty, students, and staff with university credit cards to pay for expenses, rather than relying on a reimbursement policy that disproportionately affects and punishes the poor. It would mean abolishing the gatekeeping and status hierarchies, recognizing that these, too, are rooted in anti-Black racism. It would involve administrators putting money where their mouths are about commitments to diversity, equity, and inclusion, and holding tenured faculty accountable for racism and sexism. It would mean creating workplaces that support and protect the health and well-being of students, faculty, and staff.

None of this is how the academy typically works. Instead, the academic workplace focuses on individuals, their specific achievements, and how people should navigate the winding contours of structures that were not created to support us or our work.

And I am guilty of this. I used to—and occasionally still do—write advice columns for outlets like *Inside Higher Ed* or *Medium*.

As I have spent more and more time in the profession, behind the closed doors where decisions are made, I increasingly see advice columns aimed at graduate students, postdocs, adjuncts, lecturers, and untenured faculty as misplaced and harmful. As I have gained (limited) access to power, I have witnessed the insidious ways people are excluded in the academy and how people's work, insights, and concerns are dismissed. I have been gaslighted, told by people who "respect my work" that I was wrong in all other assessments and opinions. I have been told, in more than one setting and organization, that we cannot change inequities. So, when I read advice that shifts attention away from the causes of, and potential solutions to, inequities, to what people need to understand about the "rules of the game" or how to "fit in," I get angry. The underlying premise of advice columns is that the profession cannot be changed. It can only be navigated.

It's true that this genre of writing has been helpful at revealing what's known as the "hidden curriculum," the unwritten rules and norms that structure teaching and learning and the messages people receive about what is expected and who is worthy in that setting. In effect, these columns help marginalized individuals navigate the complex and often confusing matrix that constitutes academic life.[19] I personally have benefited from them. But I also get increasingly frustrated by them. As Anthony Abraham Jack notes in his study of low-income undergraduates at an elite college, "access is not inclusion."[20]

This observation holds across academic status and rank. Individual advice on navigating racist and sexist systems may allow more people to pass through the faculty doors. But it also means that more people are traumatized, socialized into an exclusionary academic system, and taught to think that treating people in harmful ways is okay. It is not. Academia is a workplace. It needs to be at least as accountable as other work environments for the hostile climates it cultivates.

And yet, the academic system is set up to reward those who solely focus on themselves, their own careers, and their select protégés. This star system comes at the expense of building a truly inclusive community of scholars. It creates an environment actively hostile to building a just academy. This is particularly visible in the trifecta of faculty work: research, teaching, and service.

Let's start with faculty research. What would an academic justice built on Black Feminist Sociology and hope-as-a-discipline look like in the publishing process, including peer review? What would it mean to approach these processes through an ethic of care and community?

Within our own research, it means recognizing the politics of citation as "how we generate knowledge"[21] and, moreover, a form of exerting and perpetuating forms of power/knowledge.[22] It means being purposeful regarding where and from whom we center our thinking and build our communities. It necessitates that we #citeBlackwomen[23] and other scholars from a wide range of marginalized communities, whose research tends to not be published in general disciplinary journals. It requires us to orient our reading beyond those journals that are considered "top" within our own disciplines, reading widely across subfields, disciplines, and into interdisciplinary and transdisciplinary scholarship, whether in peer-reviewed journals or books or other outlets. It demands rethinking what kinds of questions, approaches, data, and writings are considered "valid." It also entails that we go back and uncover the works of scholars who have long been excluded from the academy, especially its upper echelons.[24]

Academic justice, in this respect, also means valuing failure, and not just as lessons learned on how to move forward. Rather, we must recognize that, as Jack Halberstam states, "under certain circumstances failing, losing, forgetting, unmaking, undoing, unbecoming, not knowing may in fact offer more creative, more cooperative, more surprising ways of being in the world."[25] That is, failure "provides the opportunity to use these negative affects to poke holes in the toxic positivity of contemporary life."[26] What does this have to do with academic justice in publishing? "Failing" to publish in certain journals or to receive awards, fellowships, or grants can be an indicator that one's work is unsettling presupposed expectations, rather than indicating that there's any sort of shortcoming with the project.

Our work as scholars committed to equity is to incorporate this type of "failed" research—research that doesn't fit neatly into prescribed categories—into our own research and citation politics, as well as into our teaching. It means putting into practice a commitment to valuing work that goes against the grain, against what we ourselves are often taught to do. It requires that we be committed to seeing *against* the discipline we are in, or *unseeing* and *undoing* our disciplines. And perhaps we are moving toward that goal, because despite a handful of people outwardly expressing surprise at my departure from sociology, others congratulated me and celebrated my arrival in Gender and Sexuality Studies, seeing it as freeing me from the constraints of a rigid discipline and opening up possibilities that I couldn't otherwise pursue—like this very book.

In the peer review process, academic justice means reading for possibility rather than critique. A peer review process based on care starts by reading *alongside* a given text for its contributions, value, and possibilities. Then reading it again, this time against it for the purposes of pinpointing how it can be strengthened—by which I mean not how the reviewer would write the paper, but how the author can more effectively make their arguments. And indeed, this was what I was largely trained on how to read papers and books: to focus first on contributions and potentials, to celebrate work. This training took place formally in classes, informally in how the department faculty—at the time I was there—would preface questions and comments for guest speakers and through the mentorship I received.

And they aren't the only ones. *Gender & Society*, the peer-reviewed journal for Sociologists for Women in Society, has a set of reviewer guidelines based on these principles. Its instructions, which have also been adopted by the *Sociology of Race & Ethnicity* and *Sociological Inquiry*, ask peer reviewers to start by identifying the aim of the paper before identifying any weaknesses. Reviewers are asked to "provide clear advice about how the author might address the problems you have identified or the questions you have raised." The *American Sociological Review* also asks its reviewers to begin with "big picture" comments that get at the central questions and issues of a given paper and reminds readers that assessments may differ by method used. Yet, these guidelines don't get at the racism, sexism, and other forms of discrimination that can underlie *how* people evaluate research, nor do they warn reviewers against making combative, adversarial, or overtly personal comments of or about the author.

The *Gender & Society* guidelines begin to address these latter points when they suggest that reviewers "go back through [your review] and edit out any language that seems emotionally laden or insulting. … Very occasionally, the reviewer may be so at odds with the theoretical position for which a paper is written that it is difficult to write a fair review. In this case, be honest with the editor and choose not to review it." But even these guidelines have not stopped reviewers from turning in reports that might be considered scathing, at best.

The problem may feel intractable, but multiple people and organizations have proposed multiple ways to address racism, sexism, and other forms of discrimination in the peer review process. For example, the nonprofit organization Committee on Publishing Ethics (COPE) has guidelines for editors on how to and/or whether to edit peer reviews, suggesting that editors ask reviewers to edit hostile and inappropriate comments and/or that "reviewers who decline to edit hostile or inappropriate comments or who repetitively submit reviews with such content should be informed that this is not acceptable and be removed from the reviewer pool."[27] Editors may also insert in the comments a bracket that acknowledges inappropriate and hostile comments, particularly if a journal's stance on asking peer reviewers to edit their comments is not clear.[28] These guidelines—in addition to those advising how to write a constructive review—help editors set and reinforce norms of professionalism in reviews and peer reviewers and provide accountability to those who write hostile reviews.

Making the publishing process more equitable is a continual struggle, and all actors (authors, peer reviewers, publications committees, editors) in the process need to contribute by centering pedagogies and ethics of care and challenging existing logics and frameworks.[29] This often involves extra labor, particularly on the part of the editor, who needs to create relationships of mentoring and support for authors and reviewers, reject confrontational evaluations, and actively think through how to create spaces for diverse scholarships.

These comments do not imply that we need to abolish the need to *evaluate* research. Instead, reorienting peer review toward academic justice means reimagining the relationship, purpose, and practice of the peer review and publishing process to center constructive comments aimed seeing a project's potential rather than tearing it down. A peer review based on an ethos of care is based on understanding, as author Minna Salami suggests, that "knowledge is kaleidoscopic,"[30] or that there are multiple forms of knowledge, each as "valid" as the other. Attempts to pit communities and ethics of care against "quality" only perpetuate cycles of racism, sexism, and other forms of exclusion in the peer review process.

What does an academic justice inspired by Black Feminist Sociology and hope-as-a-discipline look like in teaching and mentoring? It requires a reimagining of where teaching and mentoring rank in the hierarchy of faculty workload. At most contemporary universities, teaching and mentoring rank far behind research and publications in decisions regarding hiring, tenure, and promotion, despite their broader goal of educating students. Yet, caring about and providing resources to support research does not have to come at the expense of devaluing teaching. Indeed, the idea that teaching and research are a dichotomy, rather than complementary parts of a larger scholarly project, is part of the problem.

Our research and teaching (and service) are entwined. They inform the other. Our teaching makes us better researchers, better able to explain concepts, make connections across readings and thinkers, understand where our thinking may be difficult to follow for others, and may spark new fields of inquiry. Likewise, our research makes our teaching better, informs us of current debates in the field that we can center in the classroom and allows us to show students how knowledge is not passively produced or consume. It's actively created, and something they can, should, and need to take part in.

Academic justice also eschews uncritically reproducing the kinds of teaching we've received. Instead, a commitment to academic justice requires that we engage with pedagogical research and continued critical reflection about how we approach our students, the structure and format of our classes, as well as its substantive content.

Academic justice in the classroom means rejecting a view of students as empty vessels waiting to be filled by knowledge imparted by the instructor—what Paulo Freire refers to as the "banking" model of education, in which students are taught to receive, file, and store knowledge deposits.[31] This model stands in stark contrast to a more liberatory—and I'd add academically just—model of education where students are invited to be fully human, engage in transformative inquiry based on a critical application and creation of knowledge as "critical co-investigators in dialogue with the teacher...[who] re-considers her earlier considerations as the students express their own."[32]

Academic justice, then, entails seeing students as *partners* who bring their own embodied and learned knowledge, experiences, and voices in the classroom and seeing them as valuable members of the academy deserving of respect and consideration.[33] Academic justice also means seeing grades and assessments as mostly reflections of our own teaching methods and tools, rather than as a reflection of students and their capabilities.

What does this look like in practice and logistically? It means understanding who your students are. For example, I teach at a Hispanic-serving institution and an Asian American Native American Pacific Island-serving institution, where most students are of color, first generation, working class, are migrants, and/or come from immigrant families—students who have been particularly impacted by the COVID-19 pandemic. In this context, academic justice means taking the various traumas and disruptions of the pandemic into account when setting our expectations of what is feasible to do in our classrooms and requires flexibility.

Being thoughtful about students' needs doesn't mean "diluting" our courses, as some critics suggest. Rather, it means calibrating the format and structure of our classes to what students need to learn and why. It means thinking carefully about how best to organize class materials, lectures, assignments, and interactions to meet their needs. It means actively affirming their humanity in the content, format, structure, and even aesthetics of our classes.

Doing so means taking a lesson from what Jarvis Givens calls "fugitive pedagogy," which is "a social and rhetorical frame by which we might interpret Black Americans' pursuit to enact humanizing and affirming practices of teaching and learning."[34] Born out of the struggle of enslaved Black Americans' pursuit of "*Black*education" and liberty, fugitive pedagogy, in the words of Givens, "holds in place both the realities of constraint *and* Black Americans' constant straining against said confinement . . . Fugitivity is never one or the other . . . escape is an activity; it's not an achievement."[35] This struggle continues today in the halls of K–12 schools, in the work of Black scholars within and outside African American and Black Studies Departments, and in the everyday embodied acts for and of knowledge.

We need to understand that teaching in the pursuit of academic justice is not a thing that happens once, but rather, is an ongoing process and activity.[36] We must align the format of our classes with our principles of and commitment to learning.[37] This means thinking about how we are running our classes and whether our grading and assessments emphasize *learning* or memorization. Academic justice in teaching means centering our classes on active learning principles, how students can apply concepts to daily life, and encouraging students to be producers, not just consumers, of knowledge. It means providing students the tools they need to succeed, rather than enforcing an arbitrary, standard distribution of grades, and allowing students to revise and resubmit assignments, since this practice not only more closely mimics what happens in the "real world," but also promotes the learning of ideas.[38] Academic justice in the classroom means being open to changes, feedback, and dialogue with students.

A commitment to academic justice means centering scholars of color and other scholars who have long been marginalized from the academy in our syllabi. Not as tokens. Rather, it would mean developing course content that affirms multiple forms of knowledge production, learning and building on a rich and varied set of theoretical contributions, and seeking to transform colleges and universities whose foundations are built on exclusion, racism, sexism, and anti-Blackness. These moves are essential to transforming academic disciplines, since exclusionary foundations are traditionally most obvious in the *content* of what we teach.[39]

Teaching rooted in academic justice principles means teaching students how those exclusionary foundations get built into fields through systems of academic exchange and rewards. It means teaching the politics of citation—who gets cited and why, and how racism and sexism shapes citation counts—so that students can understand why we include and exclude certain articles and authors in our course content.[40] It's also about maintaining a humble approach to the material we teach, presenting it as the beginning of a scholarly conversation rather than as the final word on any given subject. This is the case even for graduate seminars and general examinations, which are by definition, based on a limited number of readings.

Research and teaching are, and should be, intentional and driven by purposeful decisions. There is no such thing as an "objective" and "neutral" syllabus or reading list—they are socially constructed in each class at every college and university. Collectively and individually, we must make deliberate choices in how and what we teach, choosing a path toward equity, inclusion, and an eye toward academic justice.

Finally, we might ask: What does an academic justice centered on Black Feminist Sociology and hope-as-a-discipline look like in faculty service? Faculty service tends not to count for much in tenure and promotion decisions, yet marginalized faculty are inundated with requests to serve on various professional, university, college, and departmental committees in the name of diversity. We are also continually approached by undergraduate and graduate students for shadow advising, which Ethel Tungohan described in a viral tweet, as "refer[ring] to how women—usually woc [women of color]—provide intellectual & emotional labour to students who seek them out but never recognize their labour by, say, putting them as supervisors or committee members." Or, if we are on a committee, my own experience has been at times giving even more feedback than a student receives from their chair, having students question my expertise, or having students reject my feedback, only to later incorporate it when someone else (white men, anonymous reviewers) says the same thing.

The advice column genre gives a simple and straightforward answer to the question of how marginalized faculty should respond to the deluge of requests: say no to protect our time for what counts—research. To better align priorities and time, Rockquemore and Laszloffy suggest that Black faculty switch their thinking about service, from an automatic yes and a need to come up with a reason to say no to having no be the default response and think about what they need in order to say yes.[41]

Not that saying no even works: the very people who tell you to say no to service requests will urge you to reconsider, despite your initial no. That's because departments, universities, and the academy more generally often rely on what Adia Harvey Wingfield calls racial outsourcing, or what happens "when organizations fail to do the work of transforming their culture, norms and workforces to reach communities of color and instead rely on Black professionals for this labor."[42] Since organizations, like universities and departments, rely on Black faculty and faculty of color to do the bulk of diversity work, we are asked again and again to serve, even after saying no.

And saying no just isn't an option for some of us. In their Monday Motivator emails, Kerry Ann Rockquemore, founder of the National Center for Faculty Development and Diversity (NCFDD), and Anthony Ocampo, NCFDD's academic director, acknowledge that service requests from and related to communities and students of color can "feed our souls."[43] Yet, many of us say yes because someone said yes to us. We are compelled and moved to pass it along. To further open the door and widen the path that those before us established.

The bigger problem with the advice that faculty of color "protect their time" is that, once again, it puts the onus for change on *individuals*, rather than the *system*. When implemented successfully, individual solutions mask structural problems. So, too, we should recognize that when scholars colloquially refer to teaching, mentoring, and service as "burdens"—the burden of service, the burden of teaching, the burden of mentoring—it already frames these responsibilities as negative and lesser than, when in fact, they are central to higher learning. An academic justice approach to service demands more inclusive language that recognizes service, teaching, and mentoring as important and valued work, without which we wouldn't be here. It means remembering that we wouldn't be here without the service, teaching, and mentoring that others took on for us.

Putting the responsibility for addressing unequal service expectations on the institution, rather than individuals, means that campus leadership does not ask vulnerable people to overextend themselves, rather than telling us to say no when asked. It means getting those whose nos are more likely to be heard (who tend to be white men) to say yes. It means expecting those faculty members who do not come from marginalized backgrounds to advocate for diversity, equity, and inclusion for others—though perhaps that is too lofty a goal given that these same individuals often act as obstacles to people of color in the academy. A better option, in my opinion, is for university administrators to provide summer salary or other additional financial resources to those of us who are deeply engaged in this type of work, since mentoring and service are essential to universities' continued functioning.

In 2021, I attended a book forum at the American Sociological Association's meeting for Adia Harvey Wingfield's 2019 book, *Flatlining*. In the session, Wingfield stated something to the effect that, instead of paying faculty for this work, institutions should hire separate staff to do this work. This approach would force the institution—rather than individual faculty of color—to shoulder the responsibility for what she calls in her book "equity work," or

"the various forms of labor associated with making organizations more accessible to minority communities."[44]
Diversity efforts by organizations largely do not address
the systemic processes underlying inequities, as Wingfield
herself notes.[45] One way they can, Wingfield suggests, is
for organizations to "have intentional, evidence-based ini-
tiatives in place that are designed to create both a racially
hospitable workplace for employees of color and a racially
hospitable place for the minority communities they
serve,"[46] for example by "establish[ing] or partner[ing]
with other organizations, . . . [set up] sponsorship programs for women, particularly women of color . . . enact
consequences for managers who reserve additional tasks
for workers of color and refuse to tolerate a culture where
high-status workers rely on racial stereotypes to make
assessments of minority communities."[47]

I agree with Wingfield. Although diversity programs
often fail, we still need to hold onto hope and enact
structural change within organizations. The question
becomes: How?

Some institutions have turned to mentoring to support their faculty of color. From my own experience,
however, I know that not all mentoring is equal. Many
faculty members seem to see "mentoring" as an opportunity to (re)create the toxic workplaces. That doesn't mean
that we shouldn't have mentoring programs, and, following Wingfield's recommendations, this important work
should be professionalized. But it means that in toxic

workplaces, mentoring can be another way marginalized scholars are harmed and pushed out of the academy.

Many universities have begun to emphasize mentoring and diversity, equity, and inclusion service work in faculty hiring, tenure, and promotion. This strategy involves rewarding or critiquing all faculty—regardless of their personal background—on the quality and quantity of service work they conduct. That diversity, equity, and inclusion service work needs to be everyone's responsibility—not just the responsibility of faculty of color—is important. In practice, however, even this kind of evaluation can be "spun" to benefit white men in power, for example, by focusing on the "quality" of mentorship to a few students of color, where "quality" is defined as a student's success at publishing in mainstream sociology journals. These outcomes are then contrasted with the trajectory of students who are mentored by faculty of color who may not publish (nor want to) in those same journals (perhaps, for example, they may prefer to publish in "race" journals or "ethnic studies" journals) and thus may not get jobs in disciplinary departments at research universities. Promotion committees then evaluate these faculty, and their mentorship, as "poor quality."

Every option, it seems, has drawbacks. But change is necessary. We need to use whatever power we have—on committees, in departmental meetings, in the classroom—to enact change. We cannot wait until we have tenure. Because if not now, when? My own research, teaching, and service work, within my department and university, but mostly within the profession, has been driven by this. I have committed myself to enacting change and policies (at least trying) to make a more inclusive environment, whether that means starting a mentoring program, a new award, or getting something on the table to be discussed.[48]

There will be pushback. Even so, I try and do my part, little by little, to further practices of equity. But beginning these processes and getting equity on the agenda is only the first step, and sometimes the easiest. Academic justice means recognizing the seeming impossibility of this vision and trying it anyway, knowing that hope is a discipline, a practice, an action that does not have an "end"—in the words of Mariame Kaba and Rebecca Solnit—because achieving justice is an ongoing, nonlinear process with small victories and steps backward, rather than a final destination.

And yet: I still struggle with the question of whether to leave the academy or stay. So many friends have chosen the former path. They leave because staying wasn't worth the physical, mental, and emotional pain. That was the right decision for them. I'm cautiously hopeful that staying in the academy and moving to a new department is the right decision for me, that the move allows me to continue to do the work that I love. I know that change is necessary but also gradual. But the fact that we struggle with whether to leave or stay is part of the problem. The burden of having to labor under such circumstances is itself the problem. It shouldn't be on me, or anyone else

who is an academic outsider, to have to justify or ratio-
nalize staying or, alternately, exit, when that decision is
one made under duress and a hostile work environment.

The problem is that the academy is actively excluding
us. In small and big ways. All the time. *That* is what needs
to change for us to move toward an academic justice, one
that is truly inclusive of outsiders. This change likely won't
be led by the elite graduate programs, nor by the elite
sociology journals. Instead, change begins in small acts, in
efforts to maintain integrity in each step of our responsibilities and cultivating a community of care. It begins in
how we approach our own and others' research, teaching,
and service, whether that is in our writing groups, the
peer reviews we write for journals and publishers, how we
talk about and evaluate job candidates, and how we treat
one another, with kindness and without regard to rank or
the status of our workplace. And then we must imple-
ment those acts on a larger scale, creating broader structures to nurture and support one another.

ACKNOWLEDGMENTS

This book is about being an outsider in the academy. But I would be remiss if I didn't talk about the support and mentorship I've received and without which I wouldn't be where I am. Especially from Marcela Cristina Maxfield who believed in me, had a vision, and took a risk with me. Similarly, the support from Stanford University Press staff, board, and anonymous reviewers helped give me the courage to share this book with the public. I'm grateful to have been mentored by Miguel Centeno and Viviana Zelizer. Without their guidance and support, I wouldn't have made it through graduate school. I'm also incredibly privileged in finding friends, colleagues, and mentors who've given me feedback and the courage to write this book: Rhacel Parreñas, Jean Beaman, Emmanuel David, my writing group with Amaka Okechukwu, Antonia Randolph, Zawadi Rucks-Ahidiana, Saida Grundy, and Dawn Dow, and a writing group with Brandon Robinson, Jade Sasser, Crystal Mun-hye Baik, and Randol Contreras.

Fred Wherry once told me, as I was revising my first book, that only I can write that book. Since then, I have held onto his words and grown more confident in the value of what I have to say. I'm also part of two account-ability groups, whose members helped me carve out writing time: one with Tessa Farmer, Magdalena Martinez, and Amanda Mabry-Flynn (the four of us were matched for the NCFDD Faculty Success Program and continue meeting) and the second with Rengin Firat, Kalina Michalska, and Annika Speer. The book benefited enormously from a workshop, and generative and generous comments by Anthony Ocampo, Crystal Fleming, and Jessica McCrory Calarco. Jane Ward, Bill Lopez, and Karen Levy also read draft essay(s) and provided encouragement. I'm grateful for the support I received from the Institute for Scholars & Citizens as a recipient of the Mellon Emerging Faculty Leaders Award and the UCR Center for Ideas and Society for a Project Development Grant, whose funds were matched by UCR's CHASS Dean's Office.

NOTES

PREFACE

1. While the 2020–2021 school year marked a significant decline, with 914,095 international students, there were still more international students enrolled during 2020–2021 (914,095) than in 2013–2014 (886,052). See Institute of International Education, "Enrollment Trends," https://opendoorsdata.org/data/international-students/enrollment-trends/.

2. Institute of International Education, "Number of International Students Hits All-Time High," IIE Announcement, November 18, 2019, https://www.iie.org/Why-IIE/Announcements/2019/11/Number-of-International-Students-in-the-United-States-Hits-All-Time-High.

3. Cross-Border Education Research Team, C-BERT International Campus Listing, Data originally collected by Kevin Kinser and Jason E. Lane, November 20, 2020, http://cbert.org/resources-data/intl-campus/.

4. For example, Aldon Morris, *The Scholar Denied* (Berkeley: University of California Press, 2015), Earl Wright II, *The First American School of Sociology* (London: Routledge, 2016).

5. For example, Evelyn Hu-DeHart, "The History, Development and Future of Ethnic Studies," *Phi Delta Kappan* 75,

no. 1 (1993): 50–53; see also the histories of ethnic studies departments, such as the one listed on the University of California, Berkeley's Department of Ethnic Studies "History" page: https://ethnicstudies.berkeley.edu/about/history/.

6. For example, Ghassan Moussawi, "Bad Feelings: On Trauma, Nonlinear Time, and Accidental Encounters in 'the Field,'" *Departures in Critical Qualitative Research* 10, no. 1 (2021): 78–96.

7. Kieu-Linh Caroline Valverde and Wei Ming Dariotis, "Introduction," in *Fight the Tower,* Kieu-Linh Caroline Valverde and Wei Ming Dariotis (New Brunswick, NJ: Rutgers University Press, 2020), 33–76, 45.

8. For example, Victoria Reyes, "Ethnographic Toolkit: Strategic Positionality and Researchers' Visible and Invisible Tools in Field Research," *Ethnography* 21, no 2 (2020):220–240; Randol Contreras, *The Stickup Kids* (Berkeley: University of California Press, 2012).

9. Cathy Park Hong, *Minor Feelings* (New York: One World, 2020).

10. Audre Lorde, *Sister Outsider* (Berkeley: Crossing Press, 2007 [1984]).

11. For example, Jessica McCrory Calarco, *A Field Guide to Grad School* (Princeton, NJ: Princeton University Press, 2020).

12. Christine L. Williams, *Gaslighted* (Oakland, CA: University of California Press, 2021), 94.

13. Tressie McMillan Cottom, *Thick and Other Essays* (New York: The New Press, 2019).

14. Crystal M. Fleming, *How to Be Less Stupid about Race* (Boston: Beacon Press, 2018).

15. Brittney Cooper, *Eloquent Rage* (New York: Picador, 2018).

16. Ibram X. Kendi, *How to Be an Antiracist* (New York: One World, 2019).

17. Sara Ahmed, *Living a Feminist* Life (Durham, NC: Duke University Press, 2017), 27.

ACADEMIC OUTSIDER

1. Bourdieu's body of research on field, habitus, and capital similarly portray life as a game. See for example, Pierre Bourdieu and Loïc J. D. Wacquant, *An Introduction to Reflexive Sociology* (Chicago: University of Chicago Press, 1992).

2. For example, Rosalind Chou and Joe Feagin, *The Myth of the Model Minority* (London: Routledge, 2008); Jennifer Lee and Min Zhou, *The Asian American Achievement Paradox* (New York: Russell Sage Foundation, 2015).

3. For histories of different Asian American groups in the US, see Ronald Takaki, *Strangers from a Different Shore* (Boston: Little, Brown and Company, 1998); Erika Lee, *The Making of Asian America* (New York: Simon & Schuster 2015); Helen Zia, *Asian American Dreams* (New York: Farrar, Straus and Giroux, 2001); Gary Y. Okihiro, *American History Unbound* (Berkeley: University of California Press, 2015); Frank Wu, *Yellow* (New York: Basic Books, 2002).

4. Nancy López, Edward Vargas, Melina Juarez, Lisa Cacari-Stone, and Sonia Bettez. "What's your 'Street Race'? Leveraging Multidimensional Measures of Race and Intersectionality for Examining Physical and Mental Health Status among Latinxs." *Sociology of Race and Ethnicity* 4, no. 1 (2018):49–66.

5. For additional scholarship on Filipino Americans see Rick Bonus, *Locating Filipino Americans* (Philadelphia: Temple University Press, 2000); Catherine Choy, *Empire of Care* (Durham, NC: Duke University Press, 2003); Rick Baldoz, *The Third Asiatic Invasion* (New York: NYU Press, 2011); Dawn Mabalon, *Little Manila Is in the Heart* (Durham, NC: Duke University Press, 2013).

6. Audre Lorde, *Sister Outsider* (Berkeley, CA: Crossing Press, 2007 [1984]), 116.

7. Lorde, *Sister Outsider,* 116.

8. Moya Bailey and Trudy, "On Misogynoir: Citation, Erasure, and Plagiarism," *Feminist Media Studies* 18, no. 4: 762–768.

9. Patricia Hill Collins, "Learning from the Outsider Within: The Sociological Significance of Black Feminist Thought," *Social Problems* 33, no. 6 (1986): S14–S32; Patricia Hill Collins, *Black Feminist Thought,* 2nd ed. (New York: Routledge, 2000).

10. See for example, Stuart Hall, "Introduction: Who Needs 'Identity'?" in *Questions of Cultural Identity,* ed. Stuart Hall and Paul du Gay, 1–17 (Thousand Oaks, CA: Sage, 1996); Orly Clerge, *The New Noir* (Berkeley: University of California Press, 2019).

11. José Itzigsohn and Karida Brown, *The Sociology of W.E.B. Du Bois* (New York: NYU Press, 2020).

12. W.E.B. Du Bois. *The Souls of Black Folk* (Project Gutenberg, 2021 [1903]), 1–2, https://www.gutenberg.org/files/408/408-h/408-h.htm.

13. Du Bois, *The Souls of Black Folk,* 2.

14. For distinctions about what is "marked" versus "unmarked" see, for example, Evitar Zuebravel, *Taken for Granted.* (Princeton, NJ: Princeton University Press, 2018).

15. On being Brown see José Esteban Muñoz, *The Sense of Brown* (Durham, NC: Duke University Press, 2020); On "Brown Asians" see Kevin L. Nadal, "The Brown Asian American Movement: Advocating for South Asian, Southeast Asian, and Filipino American Communities," *Asian American Policy Review* 29 (2020), https://aapr.hkspublications.org/2020/02/02/the-brown-asian-american-movement-advocating-for-south-asian-southeast-asian-and-filipino-american-communities/.

16. Neda Maghbouleh, *The Limits of Whiteness* (Stanford, CA: Stanford University Press, 2017), x.

17. Elijah Anderson, "The White Space," *Sociology of Race and Ethnicity* 1, no. 1 (2015):10–21.

18. Anderson, "The White Space," 10.

19. See for example, see Meera E. Deo, *Unequal Profession* (Stanford, CA: Stanford University Press, 2019), See pages 43–47 regarding mansplaining, hepeating, and whitesplaining.

20. Similar to Du Bois's concepts of double consciousness and veil and having to know about the white dominant world alongside his Black experiences (see also Itzigsohn and Brown, *The Sociology of W.E.B. Du Bois*); work on code- or script-switching also gets at this in a wide range of settings, e.g., Courtney McCluney, Kathrina Robotham, Serenity Lee, Richard Smith, and Myles Durkee, "The Costs of Code-Switching," *Harvard Business Review,* November 15, 2019, https://hbr.org/2019/11/the-costs-of-codeswitching; Elijah Anderson, *Code of the Street* (New York: W. W. Norton, 1999); Karyn Lacy, *Blue-Chip Black* (Berkeley: University of California Press, 2007); on similar queer navigations see Ghassan Moussawi, *Disruptive Situations* (Philadelphia: Temple University Press, 2020); Brandon Robinson, *Coming Out to the Streets* (Berkeley: University of California Press, 2020).

21. Tara J. Yosso, "Whose Culture Has Capital? A Critical Race Theory Discussion of Community Cultural Wealth," *Race, Ethnicity and Education* 8, no. 1 (2005): 69–91.

22. Allison C. Morgan, Nicholas LaBerge, Daniel B Larremore, Mirta Galesic, and Aaron Clauset, "Socioeconomic Roots of Academic Faculty," March 24, 2021, preprint in SocArXiv, 10.31235/osf.io/6wjxc.

23. Morgan et al., "Socioeconomic Roots of Academic Faculty," 5.

24. Bedelia Nicola Richards, "When Class Is Colorblind: A Race-Conscious Model for Cultural Capital Research in Education," *Sociology Compass* 14, no. 7 (2020): e12789.

25. For example, Fabio Rojas, *Grad Skool Rulz* (Smashwords Press, 2011); Karen Kelsky, *The Professor Is In* (New York: Crown, 2015); Jessica McCrory Calarco, *A Field Guide to Grad School* (Princeton, NJ: Princeton University Press, 2020); Kerry Ann Rockquemore and Tracey Laszloffy, *The Black Academic's Guide to Winning Tenure—Without Losing Your Soul* (Boulder, CO: Lynne Rienner, 2008).

26. See also Shamus Khan, *Privilege* (Princeton, NJ: Princeton University Press, 2012); Joanne W. Golann, *Scripting the Moves.* (Princeton, NJ: Princeton University Press, 2021).

27. For example, Bourdieu and Wacquant, *An Introduction to Reflexive Sociology.*

ON LOVE AND WORTH

1. For example, Elizabeth A. Armstrong, Miriam Gleckman-Krut, and Lanora Johnson, "Silence, Power and Inequality: An Intersectional Approach to Sexual Violence," *Annual Review of Sociology* 44 (2018): 99–122.

2. For example, Brandon Andrew Robinson, "Conditional Families and Lesbian, Gay, Bisexual, Transgender, and Queer Youth Homelessness: Gender, Sexuality, Family Instability, and Rejection," *Journal of Marriage and Family* 80, no. 2 (2018): 383–396; Brandon Andrew Robinson, *Coming Out to the Streets: LGBTQ Youth Experiencing Homelessness* (Berkeley: University of California Press).

3. This is a central insight from symbolic interactionism, e.g., Charles Horton Cooley, *Human Nature and the Social Order* (New York: Charles Scribner's Sons, 1922); George Herbert Mead, *Mind, Self and Society* (Chicago: University of Chicago Press, 1934); Erving Goffman, *The Presentation of Self in Everyday Life* (New York: First Anchor Books, 1934); W.E.B. Du Bois. *The Souls of Black Folk* (Project Gutenberg, 2021

[1903]), 1–2, https://www.gutenberg.org/files/408/408-h/408 -h.htm.

4. Tressie McMillan Cottom, *THICK and Other Essays* (New York: The New Press, 2019), 60.

5. For debates on whether love is an emotion and different approaches to the study of love, see Diane Felmlee and Susan Sprecher, "Love," in *Handbook of the Sociology of Emotions,* ed. Jan Stets and Jonathan Turner, 389–409 (New York: Springer, 2006).

6. Ann Swidler, *Talk of Love* (Chicago: University of Chicago Press, 2001).

7. Pierre Bourdieu, "The Forms of Capital," in *Handbook of Theory and Research for the Sociology of Education,* ed. J Richardson, 241–258 (Westport, CT: Greenwood, 1986).

8. Marci D. Cottingham, "Theorizing Emotional Capital," *Theory and Society* 45, no. 5 (2016): 451–470; Maeve O'Brien, "Gendered Capital: Emotional Capital and Mother's Care Work in Education," *British Journal of Education* 29, no. 2 (2008): 137–148; Diane Reay, "Gendering Bourdieu's Concepts of Capitals? Emotional Capital, Women and Social Class," *Sociological Review* 52, no. s2 (2004): 57–74; Diane Reay, "A Useful Extension of Bourdieu's Conceptual Framework?: Emotional Capital as a Way of Understanding Mothers' Involvement in Their Children's Education?" *Sociological Review* 48, no. 4 (2000): 568–585; Spencer E. Cahill, "Emotional Capital and Professional Socialization: The Case of Mortuary Science Students (and Me)," *Social Psychology Quarterly* 62, no. 2 (1999): 101–116; Elizabeth Vaquera, Elizabeth Aranda, and Isabel Sousa-Rodriguez, "Emotional Challenges of Undocumented Young Adults: Ontological Security, Emotional Capital, and Well-Being," *Social Problems* 64 (2017): 298–314; Carissa M. Froyum, "The Reproduction of Inequalities through Emotional Capital: The Case of Socializing Low-Income Black Girls," *Qualitative Sociology* 33 (2010): 37–54.

9. For example, Rhacel Salazar Parreñas, *Servants of Globalization* (Stanford, CA: Stanford University Press, 2015 [2001]); Valerie Francisco-Menchavez, *The Labor of Care* (Urbana: University of Illinois Press, 2018).

10. Viviana Zelizer, *The Purchase of Intimacy* (Princeton, NJ: Princeton University Press, 2005).

11. Nina Bandelj, "Relational Work and Economic Sociology," *Politics & Society* 40, no. 2 (2012): 175–201; Nina Bandelj, "Emotions in Economic Action and Interaction," *Theory and Society* 38 (2009): 347–366.

12. Bandelj, "Relational Work and Economic Sociology,"187.

13. For example, Mabel Berezin, "Secure States: Towards a Political Sociology of Emotion," *Sociological Review* 50, no. 2 suppl (2002): 33–52; James M. Jasper, "The Emotions of Protest: Affective and Reactive Emotions in and around Social Movements," *Sociological Forum* 13, no. 3 (1998): 397–424; H. J. Gans, *The War against the Poor* (New York: Basic Books, 1995); J. Soss, R. C. Fording, and S. F. Schram, *Disciplining the Poor* (Chicago: University of Chicago Press, 2011); M. Gilens, *Why Americans Hate Welfare* (Chicago: University of Chicago Press, 2009); M. B. Katz, *The Undeserving Poor* (New York: Oxford University Press, 2013); M. B. Katz, *The Undeserving Poor* (New York: Pantheon, 1989); Zawadi Rucks-Ahidiana, "Racialized Valuation and Assessments of Gentrification," Ford Foundation Conference, 2021; R. A. Moffitt, "The Deserving Poor, the Family, and the US Welfare System," *Demography* 52, no. 3 (2015): 729–749; C. D. DeSante, "Working Twice as Hard to Get Half as Far: Race, Work Ethic, and America's Deserving Poor," *American Journal of Political Science* 57, no. 2 (2013), 342–356.

14. For example, Lisa Ko, "Unwanted Sterilization and Eugenics Programs in the United States," PBS, January 29, 2016, https://www.pbs.org/independentlens/blog/unwanted-sterilization-and-eugenics-programs-in-the-united-states/.

15. Nicole Narea, "The Outcry over ICE and Hysterectomies, Explained," *Vox*, September 18, 2020, https://www.vox.com/policy-and-politics/2020/9/15/21437805/whistleblower-hysterectomies-nurse-irwin-ice.

16. Zakiya Luna, *Reproductive Rights as Human Rights* (New York: New York University Press, 2020), 45.

17. Luna, *Reproductive Rights as Human Rights,* 48.

18. Jade Sasser, *On Infertile Ground* (New York: NYU Press, 2018), 5.

19. Sasser, *On Infertile Ground,* 12

20. Du Bois, *The Souls of Black Folk*; Katrina Quisumbing King, "Recentering US Empire: A Structural Perspective on the Color Line," *Sociology of Race and Ethnicity* 5, no. 1 (2019): 11–25; see also Jean Beaman and Amy Petts, "Towards a Global Theory of Colorblindness: Comparing Colorblind Racial Ideology in France and the United States," *Sociology Compass* 14, no. 4 (2020): e12774.

21. https://www.gcclp.org/mission-vision, last accessed 12/15/2021.

22. For example, Michèle Lamont and Virág Molnár, "The Study of Boundaries in the Social Sciences," *Annual Review of Sociology* 28 (2002): 167–195.

23. For example, Jonathan Kozol, *Savage Inequalities* (New York: Harper Perennial, 1992).

24. Julie R. Posselt, *Inside Graduate Admissions* (Cambridge, MA: Harvard University Press, 2016).

25. Lauren Rivera, "Hiring as Cultural Matching: The Case of Elite Professional Service Firms," *American Sociological Review* 77, no. 6 (2012): 999–1022.

26. For example, Miller McPherson, Lynn Smith-Lovin, and James M Cook, "Birds of a Feather: Homophily in Social Networks," *Annual Review of Sociology* 27 (2001): 415–444.

27. For example, R. E. Landrum and M. A. Clump, "Departmental Search Committees and the Evaluation of Faculty Applicants," *Teaching of Psychology* 31, no. 1 (2004), 12–17.

28. R. Liera and C. Ching, "Reconceptualizing 'Merit' and 'Fit,'" in *Administration for Social Justice and Equity in Higher Education*, ed. A. Kezar and J. Posselt (New York: Routledge, 2019); L. J. Lara, "Faculty of Color Unmask Color-Blind Ideology in the Community College Faculty Search Process," *Community College Journal of Research and Practice* 43, no. 10-11 (2019) :702–717; K. O'Meara, D. Culpepper, and L. L. Templeton, "Nudging toward Diversity: Applying Behavioral Design to Faculty Hiring," *Review of Educational Research* 90, no. 3 (2020): 311–348.

29. For example, David D. Perlmutter, "A Better Way to Find 'Fit' in Academic Hiring," *Chronicle of Higher Education*, August 12, 2018, https://www.chronicle.com/article/a-better-way -to-find-fit-in-academic-hiring/; D. K. White-Lewis, "The Facade of Fit in Faculty Search Processes," *Journal of Higher Education* 91, no. 6 (2020): 850–851. Although White-Lewis does not find that "fit" is as extensively used in hiring searches, he shows how racialized evaluations of candidates lead to bias in hiring.

30. For example, scholars' assessment of quality and merit in grant proposals is shaped by self-concept, emotions, and interactions with other evaluators, see Michele Lamont, *How Professors Think* (Cambridge, MA: Harvard University Press, 2009).

31. Jane Junn and Ma'a K. Davis Cross, "Investigating Discrimination: Injustice against Women of Color in the Academy" in *Fight the Tower,* ed. Kieu-Linh Caroline Valverde and Wei Ming Dariotis, 96–109 (New Brunswick, NJ: Rutgers University Press, 2020).

32. Junn and Cross, "Investigating Discrimination," 99.

33. Zakiya Luna and Whitney N. Laster Pirtle, "Introduction," in *Black Feminist Sociology*, ed. Zakiya Luna and Whitney N Laster Pirtle, 1–16 (New York: Routledge, 2021), pp, 11.

34. For example, A. L. Duckworth, C. Peterson, M. D. Matthews, and D. R. Kelly, "Grit: Perseverance and Passion for Long-Term Goals," *Journal of Personality and Social Psychology*, 92, no. 6

(2007): 1087; A. Duckworth and J. J. Gross, "Self-Control and Grit: Related but Separable Determinants of Success," *Current Directions in Psychological Science* 23, no. 5 (2014): 319–325; K. Fosnacht, K. Copridge, and S. A. Sarraf, "How Valid Is Grit in the Postsecondary Context? A Construct and Concurrent Validity Analysis," *Research in Higher Education*, 60, no. 6 (2019): 803–822; Hye Won Kwon, "The Sociology of Grit: Exploring Grit as a Sociological Variable and Its Potential Role in Social Stratification," *Sociology Compass* 11, no. 12 (2017): e12544; For a critique of grit, see E. W. Ris, "Grit: A Short History of a Useful Concept," *Journal of Educational Controversy* 10, no. 1 (2015): 3; L. Anderson, "Lauren Anderson: Grit, Galton, and Eugenics," *Education Week Teacher*, March 21, 2014, http://blogs.edweek.org/teachers/living-in-dialogue/2014/03/lauren_anderson_grit.html.

35. Others have similarly linked love and academia. For a recent example, see Olivia Butze, "'Detoxing from Academia': One Black Scholar's Journey," *Social Science Space*, February 2019, https://www.socialsciencespace.com/2019/02/detoxing-from-academia-one-black-scholars-journey/?utm_source=twitter&utm_medium=SAGE_social&utm_content=sagesociology&utm_term=e0332592-1e4f-4c5d-98e8-d9583a7a69a3; Tressie McMillan Cottom, "I don't know who needs to hear this but it is a really good time to remember that the institution cannot love you. You don't have to pay those statements or petitions any mind, black people. Just get your hugs where you can and let them have their institution," Twitter, June 1, 2020, https://twitter.com/tressiemcphd/status/1267559834297212928?s=20&t=nM5KgsTdgF1vop_cLYxmkQ.

CONDITIONAL CITIZENSHIP

1. See Patricia Hill Collins, "Learning from the Outsider Within: The Sociological Significance of Black Feminist Thought," *Social Problems* 33, no. 6 (1986): S14–S32.

2. For example, Eric Margolis and Mary Romero, "'The Department Is Very Male, Very White, Very Old, and Very Conservative': The Functioning of the Hidden Curriculum in Graduate Sociology Departments," *Harvard Educational Review* 68, no. 1 (1998): 1–33; Mary Romero, "Reflections on '"The Department is Very Male, Very White, Very Old, and Very Conservative"': The Functioning of the Hidden Curriculum in Graduate Sociology Departments," *Social Problems* 64, no. 2 (2017): 212–218.

3. For example, Evelyn Nakano Glenn, "Structuring Citizenship: Exclusion, Subordination, and Resistance," *American Sociological Review* 76, no. 1 (2011): 1–24; Irene Bloemraad, "Theorizing and Analyzing Citizenship in Multicultural Societies," *Sociological Quarterly* 56 (2015): 591–606; Irene Bloemraad, "Theorizing the Power of Citizenship as Claims-Making," *Journal of Ethnic and Migration Studies* 44, no. 1 (2018):4–26.

4. For example, Renato Rosaldo, "Cultural Citizenship in San Jose, California," *Political and Legal Anthropology Review* 17, no. 2 (1994): 57–63.

5. Aihwa Ong, "Cultural Citizenship as Subject-Making: Immigrants Negotiate Racial and Cultural Boundaries in the United States," *Current Anthropology* 37, no. 5 (1996): 738.

6. Jean Beaman, *Citizen Outsider: Children of North African Immigrants in France* (Oakland: University of California Press, 2017).

7. Laila Lalami, *Conditional Citizens* (New York: Pantheon Books, 2020), 23.

8. For example, higher education scholar Bruce Macfarlane, *The Academic Citizen* (London: Routledge, 2007) uses the term "academic citizenship" to denote the service responsibilities of faculty.

9. For example, Gabriella Gutiérrez y Muhs, Yolanda Flores Niemann, Carmen G. González, and Angela P. Harris, *Pre-*

sumed Incompetent (Boulder: University of Colorado Press, 2012); Niemann Flores, Gabriella Yolanda Gutiérrez y Muhs, and Carmen G. González, *Presumed Incompetent II* (Logan: Utah State University Press, 2020); Michelle Harris, Sherrill L. Sellers, Orly Clerge, and Frederick W. Gooding Jr., eds., *Stories from the Front of the Room* (Lanham, MD: Rowman & Little-field, 2017); Brett C. Stockdill and Mary Yu Danico, eds., *Transforming the Ivory Tower* (Honolulu, HA: University of Hawai'i Press, 2012); Whitney N. Laster Pirtle, "We, Too, Are Academia: Demanding a Seat at the Table," *Feminist Anthropology*, online first January 27, 2021, https://doi.org/10.1002/fea2.12030; Meera E. Deo, *Unequal Profession* (Stanford, CA: Stanford University Press, 2019); Adalberto Aguirre Jr., "Women and Minority Faculty in the Academic Workplace: Recruitment, Retention, and Academic Culture," *ASHE-ERIC Higher Education Report* 27, no. 6 (2000), Jossey-Bass Higher and Adult Education Series, https://eric.ed.gov/?id=ED447752.

10. Francie Diep, "'I Was Fed Up': How #BlackInTheIvory Got Started, and What Its Founders Want to See Next," *The Chronicle,* June 9, 2020, https://www.chronicle.com/article/I-Was-Fed-Up-How/248955; see also Nidhi Subbaraman, "How #BlackInTheIvory Put a Spotlight on Racism in Academia," *Nature,* June 11, 2020, https://www.nature.com/articles/d41586-020-01741-7, among the widespread media coverage of the hashtag and the overwhelming response it received on Twitter.

11. And, to be clear, it's not limited to the academy. For a recent high-profile example, see Google's firing of Timnit Gebru and others. For her Twitter announcement, https://threadreaderapp.com/thread/1334352694664957952.html, last accessed 2/9/2021; for an article that has the original email, see https://www.platformer.news/p/the-withering-email-that-got-an-ethical.

12. Derald Wing Sue, Christina M. Capodilup, Gina C. Torino, Jennifer M. Bucceri, Aisha M. B. Holder, Kevin L. Nadal,

and Marta Esquilin, "Racial Microaggressions in Everyday Life: Implications for Clinical Practice," *American Psychologist* 62, no. 4 (2007): 273.

13. Ibram X. Kendi, *How to Be an Antiracist* (New York: One World, 2019), 47.

14. For example, Mary Romero and Eric Margolis, "Integrating Sociology: Observations on Race and Gender Relations in Sociology Graduate Programs," *Race and Society* 2, no. 1 (1999): 1–24.

15. Renato Rosaldo, "Cultural Citizenship and Educational Democracy," *Cultural Anthropology* 9, no. 3 (1994): 402–411.

16. Aldon Morris, *The Scholar Denied* (Berkeley: University of California Press, 2015).

17. For example, R. W. Connell, "Why Is Classical Theory Classical?," *American Journal of Sociology* 102, no 6 (1997): 1511–1557; Earl Wright II, "The Atlanta Sociological Laboratory 1896–1924: A Historical Account of the First American School of Sociology," *Western Journal of Black Studies* 26, no. 3 (2002); Michael Kennedy and Miguel Centeno, "Internationalism and Global Transformations in American Sociology," in *Sociology in America: A History,* ed. Craig Calhoun (Chicago: University of Chicago Press, 2008): 666–712; Julian Go, *Postcolonial Thought and Social Theory* (New York: Oxford University Press, 2016); Roderick Ferguson, *Aberrations in Black* (Minneapolis: University of Minnesota Press, 2004).

18. Victoria Reyes and Karin Johnson, "Teaching the Veil: Race, Ethnicity, and Gender in Classical Theory Courses," *Sociology of Race and Ethnicity* 6, no. 4 (2020): 562–567; Angela Fillingim and Zawadi Rucks-Ahidiana, "Theory on the Other Side of the Veil: Reckoning with Legacies of Anti-Blackness and Teaching in Social Theory," *American Sociologist* 52, no. 2 (2021): 276–303.

19. For more information about Cite Black Women, see the "Our Story" page of their website: https://www.citeblackwomen collective.org/our-story.html, last accessed 2/6/21.

20. https://gendersociety.wordpress.com/2019/06/04/does-sociology-silence-black-women/, last accessed 2/9/2021.

21. These men are perceived as white in contemporary society by many students due to their skin color, though they may have been subject to discrimination due to their class, religion, or other characteristics during the time they lived. Whiteness is a social category that is not static but has transformed over time.

22. For the text of Bylaw 55, please see: https://senate.uni versityofcalifornia.edu/bylaws-regulations/bylaws/blpart1.html ?fbclid=IwAR0JLYjvrozAAe6aIRTUUzB1Y4qXbYvBbLOUDI 58IIukH_yM3LGu98XQTMc#bl55, last accessed November 29, 2021. See, for example, the text under "C. Extension of Voting Privileges to non-Emeritae/I Faculty."

23. Carly Parnitzke Smith and Jennifer J. Freyd, "Institutional Betrayal," *American Psychologist* 69, no. 6 (2014): 578; see also: Karen D. Pyke, "Institutional Betrayal: Inequity, Discrimination, Bullying and Retaliation in the Academia," *Sociological Perspectives* 6, no. 1 (2018): 5–13; Julia S. Jordan-Zachery, "Licking Salt: A Black Woman's Tale of Betrayal, Adversity, and Survival," *Feminist Formations* 31, no. 1 (2019): 67–84; Doris Carroll, "A Faculty Woman of Color and Micro-Invalidations at a White Research Institution: A Case of Intersectionality and Institutional Betrayal," *Administrative Issues Journal* 7, no. 1 (2017): 39–50; Jennifer M. Gómez, "Microaggressions and the Enduring Mental Health Disparity: Black Americans at Risk for Institutional Betrayal," *Journal of Black Psychology* 41, no. 2 (2015): 121–143.

24. For example, Laura Hamilton and Kelly Nielsen, *Broke: The Racial Consequences of Underfunding Public Universities* (Chicago: University of Chicago Press, 2021).

25. See, for example, American Sociological Association, "Statement on Student Evaluations of Teaching," September 2019, https://www.asanet.org/sites/default/files/asa_statement _on_student_evaluations_of_teaching_feb132020.pdf.

26. Adia Harvey Wingfield and Renée Skeete Alston, "Maintaining Hierarchies in Predominately White Organizations: A Theory of Racial Tasks," *American Behavioral Scientist* 58, no. 2 (2014): 276.

27. Angela P. Harris and Carmen G. González, "Introduction," in *Presumed Incompetent,* ed. Gabriella Gutiérrez y Muhs, Yolanda Flores Niemann, Carmen G. González, and Angela P. Harris, 1–66. (Boulder: University of Colorado Press, 2012), 3; see also Harris, Sellers, Clerge, and Gooding, *Stories from the Front of the Room.*

28. For example, Marta Maria Maldonado and Katja M. Guenther, "Introduction: Critical Mobilities in the Neoliberal University," *Feminist Formations* 31, no. 1 (2019): vii–xxiii.

29. Patricia Hill Collins, *Black Feminist Thought* (New York: Routledge, 2000 [1990]), 3.

30. Ahmed, Sara, *On Being Included: Racism and Diversity in Institutional Life* (Durham, NC: Duke University Press, 2012), 22.

31. For example, Sara Ahmed, *Living a Feminist Life* (Durham, NC: Duke University Press, 2017).

32. Victor Ray, "A Theory of Racialized Organizations," *American Sociological Review* 84, no. 1 (2019): 26–53.

33. Ray, "A Theory of Racialized Organizations," 46.

34. Joan Acker, "A Theory of Gendered Organizations," *Gender and Society* 4, no. 2 (1990): 146.

35. For example, Kimberlé Crenshaw, "Mapping the Margins: Intersectionality, Identity Politics, and Violence against Women of Color," *Stanford Law Review* 43 (1990): 1241; Kimberlé Crenshaw, "Demarginalizing the Intersection of Race and Sex: A Black Feminist Critique of Antidiscrimination Doctrine, Feminist Theory and Antiracist Politics," *University of Chicago Legal Forum* (1989): 139–167; Collins, *Black Feminist Thought*; Evelyn Nakano Glenn, "From Servitude to Service

Work: Historical Continuities in the Racial Division of Paid Reproductive Labor," *Signs: Journal of Women in Culture and Society* 18, no. 1 (1992): 1–43; bell hooks, *Ain't I a Woman* (New York: Routledge, 2014 [1981]); Angela Y. Davis, *Women, Race and Class* (New York: Vintage Books, 1981); Hae Yeon Choo and Myra Marx Ferree, "Practicing Intersectionality in Sociological Research: A Critical Analysis of Inclusions, Interactions, and Institutions in the Study of Inequalities," *Sociological Theory* 28, no. 2 (2010): 129–149.

36. Joan Acker, "Inequality Regimes: Gender, Class and Race in Organizations," 20, no. 4 (2006): 443.

37. Bourdieu specifically names academia as a type of field. According to John Levin Martin, "What is Field Theory?," *American Journal of Sociology* 109, no. 1 (2003): 1–49, field theory is a family of analytic approaches. Two of the most common are Bourdieuian field theory (e.g., Pierre Bourdieu and Loïc Wacquant, *An Invitation to Reflexive Sociology* (Cambridge: Polity, 1992) and Neil Fligstein and Doug McAdam, *A Theory of Fields* (Oxford: Oxford University Press, 2012).

38. Thank you to Randol Contreras for this wording. See Cheryl I. Harris, "Whiteness as Property," *Harvard Law Review* 106, no. 8 (1993): 1707–1791 for an example of how whiteness as property has transformed to include whiteness as "neutral" and as merit. See also Crystal Mun-hye Baik, "From 'Best' to Situated and Relational: Notes toward a Decolonizing Praxis," *Oral History Review*, published online first, January 26, 2022, DOI: 10.1080/00940798.2022.2026197; Joe Feagin, *The White Racial Frame* (New York: Routledge, 2013); Eduardo Bonilla-Silva, *Racism without Racists* (Lanham, MD: Rowman & Littlefield, 2006); Michael Omi and Howard Winant, *Racial Formation in the United States* (New York: Routledge, 2014 [1986]); See Hamilton and Nielson, *Broke* on how merit in the University of California system is racialized.

39. TIAA Institute, "Taking the Measure of Faculty Diversity," Advancing Higher Education, April 2016, https://www.tiaainstitute.org/sites/default/files/presentations/2017-02/taking_the_measure_of_faculty_diversity.pdf.

40. Nancy Leong, *Identity Capitalists* (Stanford, CA: Stanford University Press, 2021).

41. For example, Jane Ward, "The Methods Gatekeepers and the Exiled Queers," in *Other, Please Specify: Queer Methods in Sociology,* ed. D'Lane Compton, Tey Meadow, and Kristen Schilt, 51–66 (Berkeley: University of California Press, 2018).

42. For two examples of research on the importance of positionality see: Collins, "Learning from the Outsider Within," S14–S32; Victoria Reyes, "Ethnographic Toolkit: Strategic Positionality and Researchers' Visible and Invisible Tools in Field Research," *Ethnography* 21, no. 2 (2020): 220–240; for one example of how positionality shapes even classical theorists, see Reyes and Johnson, "Teaching the Veil."

43. See, for example, discussions of value versus "objectivity" in Comte, Spencer, Weber, Marx. See also, Morris, *The Scholar Denied* for how this played out with regard to Du Bois.

44. Michel Foucault, *Power/Knowledge,* ed. Colin Gordon (New York: Pantheon Books, 1980); see also Patricia Hill Collins, "Moving beyond Gender: Intersectionality and Scientific Knowledge," in *Revising Gender,* ed. Myra Marx Ferree, Judith Lorber, and Beth B Hess, 259–282 (Walnut Creek, CA: Altamira Press, 2000).

45. Christine L. Williams, *Gaslighted* (Oakland, CA: University of California Press, 2021), 8–9.

46. Focus on individual or family behaviors, for example, is common in sociological research. For example, Deadric T. Williams and Regina S. Baker, "Family Structure, Risks, and Racial Stratification in Poverty," *Social Problems* 68, no. 4 (2021): 964–985.

LIVING IN PRECARITY

1. Arlie Hochschild and Anne Machung, *The Second Shift* (New York: Penguin Books, 2012 [1989]).

2. Viviana Zelizer defines care work as is a type of intimate labor based on trust and relationships which "feature sustained and/or intense personal attention that enhances the welfare of its recipients; Viviana Zelizer, *Economic Lives* (Princeton, NJ: Princeton University Press, 2011), 277

3. Caitlyn Collins, *Making Motherhood Work* (Princeton, NJ: Princeton University Press, 2019), 6.

4. See Juliann Emmons Allison, "Composing a Life in Twenty-First Century Academe: Reflections on a Mother's Challenge," *NWSA Journal* 19, no. 3 (2007): 23–46 for another example of the difficulties in academic motherhood.

5. Mary Blair-Loy, "Cultural Constructions of Family Schemas: The Case of Women in Finance," *Gender & Society* 15, no. 5 (2001): 689.

6. Shelley J. Correll, Stephen Benard, and In Paik, "Getting a Job: Is There a Motherhood Penalty?" *American Journal of Sociology* 112, no. 5 (2007): 1297–1338.

7. Joan Williams, *Unbending Gender* (Oxford: Oxford University Press, 2000), 70.

8. For a more optimistic view on navigating motherhood in academia see Kelly Ward and Lisa Wolf-Wendel, *Academic Motherhood* (New Brunswick, NJ: Rutgers University Press, 2012).

9. For example, Danielle J. Lindemann, *Commuter Spouses* (Ithaca, NY: Cornell University Press, 2019).

10. Dawn Marie Dow, *Mothering While Black* (Berkeley: University of California Press, 2019), 15.

11. For example, Kelley Bedard Antecol and Jenna Stearns, "Equal but Inequitable: Who Benefits from Gender-Neutral Tenure Clock Stopping Policies?" *American Economic Review* 108, no. 9 (2018): 2420–2441.

12. Collen Flaherty Manchester, Lisa M. Leslie, and Amit Kramer, "Is the Clock Still Ticking? An Evaluation of the Consequences of Stopping the Tenure Clock," *ILR Review* 66, no. 1 (2013): 3–31.

13. See Collins, *Making Motherhood Work*.

14. Collins, 7.

15. David Brady, "Theories of the Causes of Poverty," *Annual Review of Sociology* 45 (2019): 155–175, see 164. Brady compares individual, structural, and political theories of the causes of poverty. Here I'm quoting from the political theories.

16. Charles Tilly, *Durable Inequality* (Berkeley: University of California Press, 1998), 6.

17. For example, W.E.B. Du Bois. The Souls of Black Folk (Project Gutenberg, 2021 [1903]), https://www.gutenberg.org/files/408/408-h/408-h.htm; Katrina Quisumbing King, "Recentering US Empire: A Structural Perspective on the Color Line," *Sociology of Race and Ethnicity* 5, no. 1 (2019): 11–25; Jean Beaman and Amy Petts, "Towards a Global Theory of Colorblindness: Comparing Colorblind Racial Ideology in France and the United States," *Sociology Compass* 14, no. 4 (2020): e12774.

18. Peter Evans, *Dependent Development* (Princeton, NJ: Princeton University Press, 1979).

19. Cedric J. Robinson, *Black Marxism* (Chapel Hill: University of North Carolina Press, 2000 [1983]). See also Jordanna Matlon, "Racial Capitalism and the Crisis of Black Masculinity," *American Sociological Review* 81, no. 5 (2016): 1014–1038.

20. See also the long history of work on dependency and world-systems theories, including the body of work from contemporary classical theorists in this area such as Giovanni Arrighi, Christopher Chase-Dunn, Immanuel Wallerstein, Beverly Silver, Samir Amin, Han Singer, Raúl Prebisch, and Walden Bello, among others.

21. Richard Rothstein, *The Color of Law* (New York: Liveright, 2017); see also Douglas S. Massey and Nancy A. Denton,

American Apartheid (Cambridge, MA: Harvard University Press, 1993).

22. Bea Waterfield, Brenda L. Beagan, and Tameera Mohamed, "'You Always Remain Slightly an Outsider': Experiences of Academics from Working-Class or Improvised Backgrounds," *Canadian Review of Sociology* 56, no. 3 (2019): 368–388 refers to working-class academics as "cultural outsiders."

23. Arne L. Kalleberg and Steven P. Vallas, "Probing Precarious Work: Theory, Research and Politics," *Research in the Sociology of Work* 31 (2018): 1.

24. American Association of University Professors Research Office, "Trends in Academic Labor Force, 1975–2015," March 2017, https://wwwaauporg/sites/default/files/Academic_Labor _Force_Trends_1975-2015pdf.

25. ASA Task Force on Contingent Faculty Employment, "Contingent Faculty Employment in Sociology," January 2019, https://wwwasanetorg/sites/default/files/asa_tf_on_contingent _faculty_final_reportpdf.

26. Theresa O'Keefe and Aline Courtois, "'Not One of the Family': Gender and Precarious Work in the Neoliberal University," *Gender, Work, and Organization* 26 (2019): 463–479.

27. TIAA Institute, "Taking the Measure of Faculty Diversity," Advancing Higher Education, April 2016, https://www .tiaainstituteorg/sites/default/files/presentations/2017-02/taking _the_measure_of_faculty_diversitypdf.

28. For example, O'Keefe and Courtois, "'Not One of the Family'"; Mariya Ivancheva, Kathleen Lynch, and Kathryn Keating, "Precarity, Gender and Care in the Neoliberal Academy," *Gender, Work and Organization* 26 (2019): 448–462.

29. For example, Melanie Hanson, "Student Loan Debt Statistics," Education Data Initiative, January 27, 2022, https:// educationdataorg/student-loan-debt-statistics.

30. Abigail Hess, "Survey: Student Loan Holders Are More Likely to Be Women and People of Color," NBC News,

January 28, 2022, https://wwwnbcnewscom/news/nbcblk/survey-student-loan-holders-are-likely-women-people-color-rcna13962.

31. Laura Hamilton and Kelly Nielsen, *Broke: The Racial Consequences of Underfunding Public Universities* (Chicago: University of Chicago Press, 2021).

32. Hamilton and Nielsen, *Broke*, 15.

33. See also Teresa Watanabe, "UC Riverside Has High Share of Underserved Students but Funding Gap Prompts Equity Debate," *Los Angeles Times,* April 8, 2021.

34. Many women of color, particularly but not limited to immigrants, also often have additional financial responsibilities for supporting extended families who may or may not live with them or even within the U.S. For example, the Philippines relies extensively on remittances from family who live and work elsewhere. Quoting officials from the Bangko Sentral ng Pilipinas, the *Manila Times* reported that, in 2019, "OFW [overseas Filipino workers] remittances accounted for 9.3 percent and 7.8 percent of the gross domestic product and gross national income [in the Philippines]." Mayvelin U. Caraballo, February 18, 2020, "OFW Remittances Hit All-Time High in 2019," https://www.manilatimes.net/2020/02/18/news/national/ofw-remittances-hit-all-time-high-in-2019/688077/. This number likely underestimates the value of remittances sent to the Philippines, as Filipino overseas workers are just one group of people who send money back home. Second-generation Filipino Americans, for example, also send remittances, as well as other goods, to the Philippines. See, for example, Armand Gutierrez, "The Determinants of Remittances among Second-Generation Mexican- and Filipino-Americans," *Ethnic and Racial Studies* 43, no. 9 (2020): 1711–1731; Armand Gutierrez, "A Family Affair: How and Why Second-Generation Filipino-Americans Engage in Transnational Connections," *Ethnic and Racial Studies* 41, no. 2 (2018): 229–247.

35. Frederick Wherry, Kristin Seefeldt, and Anthony Alvarez, *Credit Where It's Due* (New York: Russell Sage Foundation, 2019), 7.

36. Wherry, Seefeldt, and Alvarez, *Credit Where It's Due,* 16

37. See Viviana Zelizer, *The Purchase of Intimacy* (Princeton, NJ: Princeton University Press, 2005) on intimacy, where intimate relations are those "relationships [where] at least one person is committing trust and at least one person has access to information or attention that, if made widely available, would damage the other" (15).

38. For example, Tim Hallett, "The Myth Incarnate: Recoupling Processes, Turmoil, and Inhabited Institutions in an Urban Elementary School," *American Sociological Review* 75, no. 1 (2010): 52–74; Tim Hallett and Marc J. Ventresca, "Inhabited Institutions: Social Interactions and Organizational Forms in Gouldner's *Patterns of Industrial Bureaucracy,*" *Theory and Society* 35 (2006): 213–236.

OVERLAPPING SHIFTS AND COVID-19

1. "Elder sister" in Tagalog.

2. For research on children, see for example: Maria Spinelli, Francesca Lionetti, Annalisa Setti, and Mirco Fasolo, "Parenting Stress during the COVID-19 Outbreak: Socioeconomic and Environmental Risk Factors and Implications for Children Emotion Regulation," *Family Process* 60, no. 2 (2021): 639–653; Mara Morelli, Elena Cattelino, Roberto Baiocco, Carmen Trumello, Alessandra Babore, Carla Candelori, and Antonio Chirumbolo, "Parents and Children during the COVID-19 Lockdown: The Influence of Parenting Distress and Parenting Self-Efficacy on Children's Emotional Well-Being," *Frontiers in Psychology* 11 (2020): 2584.

3. Andrea O'Reilly describes the "the emotional and intellectual labour of mother work" (8) as the "third shift" and "the

homeschooling of children" (8) as the fourth shift during COVID, separating out two forms of care work (mother work and homeschooling) that usually fall under the term "second shift" alongside housekeeping responsibilities. See Andrea O'Reilly, "'Trying to Function in the Unfunctionable': Mothers and COVID-19" *Journal of the Motherhood Initiative for Research and Community Involvement* 11, no. 1 (2020): 7–24.

4. Sarah Crook, "Parenting during the COVID-19 Pandemic of 2020: Academia, Labour and Care Work," *Women's History Review* 29, no 7 (2020):1226–1238 calls this in her abstract the "concurrent 'double shift.'"

5. For example, Caitlyn Collins, Liana Christin Landivar, Leah Ruppanner, and William J. Scarborough, "COVID-19 and the Gender Gap in Work Hours," *Gender, Work & Organizations,* published online first July 2, 2020, https://doi.org/10.1111/gwao.12506, last accessed 9/30/3030; Suzanne M. Edwards and Larry Snyder, "Yes, Balancing Work and Parenting Is Impossible. Here's the Data," *Washington Post*, July 10, 2020, https://www.washingtonpost.com/outlook/interruptions-parenting-pandemic-work-home/2020/07/09/599032e6-b4ca-11ea-aca5-ebb63d27e1ff_story.html; E. J. Dickson, "Coronavirus Is Killing the Working Mother," *Rolling Stone*, July 3, 2020, https://www.rollingstone.com/culture/culture-features/working-motherhood-covid-19-coronavirus-1023609/; Misty L. Heggeness and Jason M. Fields, "Working Moms Bear Brunt of Home Schooling while Working During COVID-19," US Census, August 18, 2020, https://www.census.gov/library/stories/2020/08/parents-juggle-work-and-child-care-during-pandemic.html; Alison Andrew, Sarah Cattan, Monica Costa Dias, Christine Farquharson, Lucy Kraftman, Sonya Krutikova, Angus Phimister, and Almudena Sevilla, "The Gendered Division of Paid and Domestic Work under Lockdown," *IZA DP No. 13500,* July 2020, http://ftp.iza.org/dp13500.pdf; Caitlyn

Collins, Leah Ruppanner, Liana Christin Landivar, and William J. Scarborough, "The Gendered Consequences of a Weak Infrastructure of Care: School Reopening Plans and Parents' Employment During the COVID-19 Pandemic," *Gender & Society* 35, no. 2 (2021): 180–193; Nino Bariola and Caityln Collins, "The Gendered Politics of Pandemic Relief: Labor and Family Policies in Denmark, Germany, and the United States During COVID-19," *American Behavioral Scientist* 65, no. 12 (2021): 1671–1697; Jessica McCrory Calarco, Emily Meanwell, Elizabeth M. Anderson, and Amelia S. Knopf, "By Default: How Mothers in Different-Sex Dual-Earner Couples Account for Inequalities in Pandemic Parenting," *Socius* 7 (2021): 1–15; Daniela Marchetti, Lilybeth Fontanesi, Cristina Mazza, Serena Di Giandomenico, Paolo Roma, and Maria Cristina Verrocchio, "Parenting-Related Exhaustion during the Italian COVID-19," *Journal of Pediatric Psychology* 45, no. 10 (2020): 1114–1123; Shawna J. Lee, Kaitlin P. Ward, Olivia D. Chang, and Kasey M. Downing, "Parenting Activities and the Transition to Home-Based Education during the COVID-19 Pandemic," *Children and Youth Services Review* 122 (2021): 105585; Joyce Weeland, Loes Keijsers, and Susan Branje, "Introduction to the Special Issue: Parenting and Family Dynamics in Times of COVID-19 Pandemic," *Developmental Psychology* 57, no. 10 (2021): 1559–1562; Margaret L. Kerr, Hannah F. Rasmussen, Kerrie A. Fanning, and Sarah M. Braaten, "Parenting during COVID-19: A Study of Parents' Experiences across Gender and Income Levels," *Family Relations* 70 (2021): 1327–1342; Richard J. Petts, Daniel L. Carlson, and Joanna R. Pepin, "A Gendered Pandemic: Childcare, Homeschooling, and Parents' Employment during COVID-19," *Gender, Work & Organization* 28 (2021): 515–534; for research on academic parents in particular, see Sara Crook, "Parenting during the COVID-19 Pandemic of 2020: Academia, Labour and Care Work," *Women's*

History Review 29, no. 7 (2020): 1226–1238; Marta Kowal, Piotr Sorokowski, Agnieszka Sorokowska, Isabela Lebuda, Agata Groyecka-Bernard, Michał Białek, Kaja Kowalska, Lidia Wojtycka, Alicja M. Olszewska, and Maciej Karwowski, "Dread in Academia—How COVID-19 Affects Science and Scientists," *Anthropological Review* 83, no. 4 (2020): 387–394; Brooke Peterson Gabster, Kim van Daalen, Roopa Dhatt, and Michele Barry, "Challenges for the Female Academic during the COVID-19 Pandemic," *Lancet* 395 (2020): 1968–1970; Fernanda Staniscuaski et al., "Impact of COVID-19 on Academic Mothers" (Letter), *Science* 368, no. 6492 (2020): 724; Rodrigo Rosa, "The Trouble with 'Work–Life Balance' in Neoliberal Academia: A Systematic and Critical Review," *Journal of Gender Studies* 31, no. 1 (2022): 55–73; Megha Anwer, "Academic Labor and the Global Pandemic: Revisiting Life-Work Balance under COVID-19," *Susan Bulkeley Butler Center for Leadership Excellence and ADVANCE Working Paper Series* 3, no. 1 (2020): 5–13.

6. Punit Renjen, "Women Are Vanishing from the Workplace—Here's How to Bring Them Back," The Hill, June 13, 2021, https://thehill.com/opinion/campaign/558180-women-are-vanishing-from-the-workplace-heres-how-to-bring-them-back.

7. Renjen, "Women Are Vanishing from the Workplace."

8. For example, Katie L. Acosta, "Racism: A Public Health Crisis," *City & Community*, published online first September 4, 2020, https://onlinelibrary.wiley.com/doi/full/10.1111/cico.12518.

9. Jean Beaman, "Underlying Conditions: Global Anti-Blackness Amid COVID-19," *City & Community*, published online first September 1, 2020, https://onlinelibrary.wiley.com/doi/full/10.1111/cico.12519, p. 2, italicized in original.

10. Whitney N. Laster Pirtle, "Racial Capitalism: A Fundamental Cause of Novel Coronavirus (COVID-19) Pandemic Inequities in the United States," *Health Education & Behavior* 47, no. 4 (2020): 504–508.

11. W. N. Laster Pirtle and T. Wright, "Structural Gendered Racism Revealed in Pandemic Times: Intersectional Approaches to Understanding Race and Gender Health Inequities in COVID-19," *Gender & Society* 35, no. 2 (2021): 171.

12. For example, Mayo Clinic, "Stress Symptoms: Effects on Your Body and Behavior," April 4, 2019, https://www.mayoclinic.org/healthy-lifestyle/stress-management/in-depth/stress-symptoms/art-20050987; for information on health problems of Asian American women in the academy, see Kieu Linh Caroline Valverde, Cara Maffini Pham, Melody Yee, and Jing Mai, "Killing Machine: Exposing the Health Threats to Asian American Women Scholars in Academia," in *Fight the Tower*, ed. Kieu Linh Caroline Valverde and Wei Ming Dariotis, 110–160 (New Brunswick, NJ: Rutgers University Press).

13. For one example of the health effects of living in what they call "lethally surveilled neighborhoods," see Alyasah Alii Sewell, Justin M. Feldman, Rashawn Ray, Keon L. Gilbert, Kevin A. Jefferson, and Hedwig Lee, *Ethnic and Racial Studies*, published online first July 22, 2020, https://www.tandfonline.com/doi/full/10.1080/01419870.2020.1781913, last accessed 9/30/2020.

14. For an example of research on how stigma, prejudice, and health relate, see Jennifer Stuber, Ilan Meyer, and Bruce Link, "Stigma, Prejudice, Discrimination, and Health," *Social Science & Medicine* 67, no. 3 (2008): 351–357 and the accompanying articles in the special issue.

15. Marta Kowal et al., "Dread in Academia," 387–394; Brooke Peterson Gabster et al., "Challenges for the Female Academic during the COVID-19 Pandemic," 1968–1970.

16. For example, Dessie Clark, Ethel L. Mickey, and Joya Misra, "Reflections on Institutional Equity for Faculty in Response to COVID-19," *Susan Bulkeley Butler Center for Leadership Excellence and ADVANCE Working Paper Series* 3, no. 2 (2020); Joya Misra, Ethel L. Mickey, and Dessie Clark,

"Implementing Pandemic Equity Measures for Faculty," *Inside Higher Ed*, May 27, 2021, https://www.insidehighered.com/advice/2021/05/27/four-steps-institutional-leaders-should-take-create-equitable-systems-faculty; Joya Misra, Dessie Clark, and Ethel L. Mickey, "Keeping COVID-19 From Sidelining Equity," *Inside Higher Ed*, February 10, 2021, https://www.inside highered.com/views/2021/02/10/without-intentional-interventions -pandemic-will-make-higher-education-less-diverse; Ethel L. Mickey, Dessie Clark, and Joya Misra, "Measures to Support Faculty During COVID-19," *Inside Higher Ed*, September 4, 2020, https://www.insidehighered.com/advice/2020/09/04/advice-academic-administrators-how-best-support-faculty-during -pandemic-opinion; Jessica L. Malisch et al. "In the Wake of COVID-19, Academia Needs New Solutions to Ensure Gender Equity" (opinion), *PNAS* 117, no. 27 (2020): 15378–15381.

17. For example, Flaminio Squazzoni, Giangiacomo Bravo, Francisco Grimaldo, Daniel García-Costa, Mike Farjam, and Bahar Mehmani, "Gender Gap in Journal Submissions and Peer Review during the First Wave of the COVID-19 Pandemic. A Study on 2329 Elsevier Journals," *PLoS ONE* 16 no. 10 (2021): e0257919, https://doi.org/10.1371/journal.pone.0257919.

18. Squazzoni et al, "Gender Gap in Journal Submissions."

19. "As US Nears 800,000 Virus Deaths, 1 of Every 100 Older Americans Has Perished," *New York Times* December 13, 2021, https://www.nytimes.com/2021/12/13/us/covid-deaths -elderly-americans.html.

20. For similar insights see Brittney Cooper, *Eloquent Rage* (New York: Picador, 2018).

21. UMass ADVANCE, "Documenting Pandemic Impacts: Best Practices," 2020, accessed December 17, 2021, https://www .umass.edu/advance/sites/default/files/inlinefiles/UMass%20 ADVANCE%20COVID-19%20Tool%20July%2027%202020 %20Final.pdf.

22. BlackPast, "(1857) Frederick Douglass, 'If There Is No Struggle, There Is No Progress,'" BlackPast.org., https://www.blackpast.org/african-american-history/1857-frederick-douglass-if-there-no-struggle-there-no-progress/.

23. Lorde, *Sister Outsider*, 124, 128–129.

24. Centers for Disease Control and Prevention, "1918 Pandemic (H1N1virus)," https://www.cdc.gov/flu/pandemic-resources/1918-pandemic-h1n1.html, last accessed 9/30/2020.

25. For example, Maegan Vazquez and Paul LeBlanc, "Trump Refuses to Condemn White Supremacists at Presidential Debate," CNN, September 30, 2020, https://www.cnn.com/2020/09/30/politics/proud-boys-trump-white-supremacists-debate/index.html.

ACADEMIC JUSTICE

1. Brandon Robinson, "Non-Binary Embodiment, Queer Knowledge Production, and Disrupting the Cisnormative Field: Notes from a Trans Ethnographer," *Journal of Men's Studies,* forthcoming; Jane Ward, "The Methods Gatekeepers and the Exiled Queers," in *Other, Please Specify,* ed. D'Lane Compton, Tey Meadow, and Kristen Schilt (Berkeley: University of California Press, 2018), 51–66; Marta Maria Maldonado and Katja Guenther, "Introduction: Critical Mobilities in the Neoliberal University," *Feminist Formations* 31, no. 1 (2019): vii–xxiii; Mary Romero, "Sociology Engaged in Social Justice," *American Sociological Review* 85, no. 1 (2020): 1–30.

2. Of course, interdisciplinary departments are not immune to racism and/or sexism; for example, gender studies long centered on white feminism, Ruby Hamad, *White Tears/Brown Scars* (New York: Catapult, 2020); Lorde, *Sister Outsider*, Patti Duncan, "Hot Commodities, Cheap Labor: Women of Color in the Academy," *Frontiers* 35, no. 3 (2014): 39–63.

3. For an example of recent threats to cut back these inter-disciplinary departments, see Dave Bangert, "Purdue Reverses Cuts to African American, Women's Studies, among Others, on the Eve of Creating Diversity Task Force," *Lafayette Journal & Courier*, August 6, 2020, https://www.jconline.com/story/news/2020/08/06/purdue-reverses-cuts-african-american-womens-studies-among-others-eve-creating-diversity-task-force/3307231001/. See also recent bans on teaching critical race studies: Rashawn Ray and Alexandra Gibbons, "Why Are States Banning Critical Race Theory?" *Brookings,* November 2021, https://www.brookings.edu/blog/fixgov/2021/07/02/why-are-states-banning-critical-race-theory/; the outrage over Nikole Hannah-Jones's 1619 Project and her denial of tenure at University of North Carolina, Chapel Hill: Nikole Hannah-Jones, "Nikole Hannah-Jones Issues Statement on Decision to Decline Tenure Offer at University of North Carolina-Chapel Hill and to Accept Knight Chair Appointment at Howard University," NAACP Legal Defense and Educational Fund, July 6, 2021, https://www.naacpldf.org/press-release/nikole-hannah-jones-issues-statement-on-decision-to-decline-tenure-offer-at-university-of-north-carolina-chapel-hill-and-to-accept-knight-chair-appointment-at-howard-university/, among many others.

4. Adia Harvey Wingfield, *Flatlining: Race, Work, and Health Care in the New Economy* (Berkeley: University of California Press, 2019), 7.

5. Sara Ahmed, *Living a Feminist Life* (Durham, NC: Duke University Press, 2017), 2.

6. https://towardfreedom.org/story/archives/activism/hope-is-a-discipline/

7. Rebecca Solnit, *Hope in the Dark: Untold Histories, Wild Possibilities* (Chicago: Haymarket Books, 2016 [2004]), xiv; see also Cooper, *Eloquent Rage*, 274.

8. For one example, see the 2020 Sociologists for Women in Society Committee on Academic Justice report: https://socwomen.org/about/https-socwomen-org-about-academicjustice/.

9. This draws on similar popular and scholarly understandings of social justice and racial justice in the academy, e.g., Romero, "Sociology Engaged in Social Justice" for an example of narratives of how to overcome and address inequities in academia see Manya Whitaker and Eric Anthony Grollman, eds., *Counternarratives from Women of Color Academics* (New York: Routledge, 2019).

10. Maegan Parker Brooks and Davis Houck, eds., *Speeches of Fannie Lou Hamer* (Jackson: University Press of Mississippi, 1971).

11. Luna and Pirtle, *Black Feminist Sociology*, 6.

12. Luna and Pirtle, 8

13. Toni Morrison, *The Source of Self-Regard* (New York: Alfred A Knopf, 2019), 111.

14. bell hooks, *All about Love* (New York: William Morrow, 2001), 6.

15. hooks, *All about Love*,77.

16. hooks, 30.

17. hooks, 87.

18. bell hooks, *Teaching Critical Thinking* (New York: Routledge, 2010), 32.

19. There are helpful resources on navigating different aspects of academic life, including the National Center for Faculty Diversity and Development, advice columns at Inside Higher Ed (in particular, its Conditionally Accepted column) and Chronicle of Higher Education; helpful websites such as Tanya Golash-Boza's *Get a Life, PhD*, Zawadi Rucks Ahidiana-Massac's *Practical PhD*, Karen Kelsky's *The Professor Is In*, Mirya Holman's *Aggressive Winning Scholars Newsletter*, and books such as Calarco, *A Field Guide to Grad School;* Rojas,

Grad Skool Rulz; Rockquemore and Laszloffy, *The Black Academic's Guide to Winning Tenure—Without Losing Your Soul.* There are also countless books on how to write dissertations, articles, or grants and on transforming your dissertation into a book. I have used many of these resources. My point is that it is exhausting to always be told more advice on how to navigate a structure, rather than changing those structures.

20. Anthony Abraham Jack, *The Privileged Poor* (Cambridge, MA: Harvard University Press, 2019), 24.

21. Ahmed, *Living a Feminist Life*, 14.

22. Foucault, *Power/Knowledge.*

23. For example, Christen A. Smith, Erica L. Williams, Imani A. Wadud, Whitney N. L. Pirtle, the Cite Black Women Collective, "Cite Black Women: A Critical Praxis (A Statement)," *Feminist Anthropology* 2, no. 1 (2021): 10–17.

24. E.g., Victoria Reyes, "For a Du Boisian Economic Sociology," *Sociology Compass*, online first March 24, 2022, https://doi.org/10.1111/soc4.12975.

25. Jack Halberstam, *The Queer Art of Failure* (Durham, NC: Duke University Press, 2011), 2–3.

26. Halberstam, *The Queer Art of Failure*, 3.

27. Committee on Publishing Ethics, "Guidelines: Editing Peer Review," p. 4, 2021, https://publicationethics.org/files/editing-peer-reviews-cope-guideline.pdf.

28. Committee on Publishing Ethics, "Guidelines: Editing Peer Review," p. 5, https://publicationethics.org/files/editing-peer-reviews-cope-guideline.pdf.

29. For a detailed approach, see Mohan J. Dutta, "Dismantling Disciplinary Whiteness: Centering Care in Editorial Stewardship," National Center for Faculty Development and Diversity (NCFDD) webinar, October 19, 2021.

30. Minna Salami, *Sensuous Knowledge* (New York: Amistad, 2020), 21.

31. Paulo Freire, *Pedagogy of the Oppressed* (New York: Bloomsbury Academic, 2018 [1970]), see chapter 2.

32. Freire, *Pedagogy of the Oppressed,* 81.

33. See the work of Alison Cook-Sather and the Teaching and Learning Institute at Bryn Mawr College and Haverford College, https://tli-resources.digital.brynmawr.edu, last accessed 1/2/21; Rick Bonus, *The Ocean in the School* (Durham, NC: Duke University Press, 2020); Tara Yosso, "Whose Culture Has Capital? A Critical Race Theory Discussion of Community Cultural Wealth," *Race, Ethnicity and Education* 8, no. 1 (2005): 69–91.

34. Jarvis Givens, *Fugitive Pedagogy* (Cambridge, MA: Harvard University Press, 2021), 11.

35. Givens, *Fugitive Pedagogy*, 15.

36. For example, Susan A. Ambrose, Michael W. Bridges, Michele DiPietro, Marsha C. Lovett, and Marie K. Norman, *How Learning Works* (San Francisco: Jossey-Bass, 2010).

37. For additional work on pedagogical approaches, see Ken Bain, *What the Best College Teachers Do* (Cambridge, MA: Harvard University Press, 2004); hooks, *Teaching Critical Thinking*; Stephen Brookfield, *Becoming a Critically Reflective Teacher* (San Francisco: Jossey-Bass, 2017); Darby Flower with James M. Lang, *Small Teaching Online* (San Francisco: Jossey-Bass, 2019); Aimi Hamraie, "Accessible Teaching in the time of COVID-19," *Mapping Access*, March 10, 2020, https://www.mapping-access.com /blog-1/2020/3/10/accessible-teaching-in-the-time-of-covid-19.

38. For example, Craig E. Nelson, "Dysfunctional Illusions of Rigor: Lessons from the Scholarship of Teaching and Learning," in *To Improve the Academy*, ed. Linda B. Nilson and Judith E. Miller (San Francisco: Jossey-Bass, 2010).

39. Morris, *The Scholar Denied*; Connell, "Why Is Classical Theory Classical?," Wright, "The Atlanta Sociological Laboratory 1896–1924."

40. Reyes and Johnson, "Teaching the Veil"; Meredith D. Clark, "Remaking the #Syllabus: Crowdsourcing Resistance Praxis as Critical Public Pedagogy," *Communication, Culture & Critique* 13 (2020): 222–241; Milton A. Fuentes, David G. Zelaya, and Joshua W. Madsen, "Rethinking the Course Syllabus: Considerations for Promoting Equity, Diversity, and Inclusion," *Teaching of Psychology* 48, no. 1 (2021):69–79.

41. Rockquemore and Laszloffy, *The Black Academic's Guide to Winning Tenure—Without Losing Your Soul.*

42. Wingfield, *Flatlining*, 34

43. For example, see the NCFDD Monday Motivator email on September 21, 2020, "Saying 'No' at Mid-Career."

44. Wingfield, *Flatlining*, 34

45. Wingfield, *Flatlining*; see also Frank Dobbin and Alexandra Kalev, "Why Diversity Programs Fail," *Harvard Business Review* 94, no. 7 (2016); Alexandra Kalev, Frank Dobbin, and Erin Kelly, "Best Practices or Best Guesses? Assessing the Efficacy of Corporate Affirmative Action and Diversity Policies," *American Sociological Review* 71, no. 4 (2006): 589–617; Ahmed, *On Being Included*; Ellen Berrey, *The Enigma of Diversity* (Chicago: University of Chicago Press, 2015).

46. Wingfield, *Flatlining*, 171.

47. Wingfield, *Flatlining*, 172–173.

48. Agenda-setting is one of the faces of power, see Steven Lukes, *Power* (London: Red Globe Press, 2005 [1974]).